The Apostolic Entrepreneur

By Les D. Crause

The Apostolic Entrepreneur

Copyright © 2015 by Global Business Ministries International
All rights reserved
5663 Balboa Ave #416,
San Diego,
California 92111,
United States of America

1st Printing August 2015

Printed by **CreateSpace, an Amazon.com Company**
Published by **Global Business Ministries International**
E-mail Address: admin@gbm-i.com
Web Address: www.gbm-bookshop.com

All rights reserved under International Copyright Law. Contents may not be reproduced in whole or in part in any form without the express written consent of the publisher.

Scripture quotations are taken from the Global Business Ministries Version (GBMV) of the Bible.

Contents

Section 01 - The Roads of Ministry and Business 8
Chapter 01 – A Different Kind of End Times Church 8
Chapter 02 - Ministry Calling Versus Business Calling 18
Chapter 03 – Ministry and Business Working Together . 30
Section 02 - The Preparation of an Entrepreneur 42
Chapter 04 – Preparation in the Work Place 42
Chapter 05 – Rising Up in the Work Place 56
Chapter 06 – Standing On My Own in Business 64
Chapter 07 - Preparation of Fivefold Entrepreneurs 78
Section 03 - The Training of an Entrepreneur 98
Chapter 08 – The Phases of Training 98
Chapter 09 - Things You Must Let Go Of 106
Chapter 10 - Four Entrepreneurs from Scripture 122
Section 04 – The Business Anointing 146
Chapter 11 – What the Business Anointing is 146
Chapter 12 – An Anointing for Business Success 158
Chapter 13 – Ministry and Business Flowing Together 170
Section 05 - The Fivefold Entrepreneur 184
Chapter 14 – Different Types of Business Entrepreneurs
.... 184
Chapter 15 – Business Training for Evangelists, Pastors and Teachers 202
Chapter 16 – Business Training for Prophets and Apostles
.... 222
Section 06 - The Sevenfold Apostolic Leaders 236
Chapter 17 – Business and Ministry Apostles Together
.... 236
Chapter 18 – How the Business Apostles Will Function
.... 246

Section 07 - Cost of the Apostolic Business Calling 268
Chapter 19 – Letting Go of Your Archetypes 268
Chapter 20 – Letting Go of Your Family........................280
Chapter 21 – Letting Go of Titles and Offices...............292
Chapter 22 - What You Will Keep 302
Chapter 23 – Price the Four Entrepreneurs Paid..........310

Section 01 - The Roads of Ministry and Business

CHAPTER 01

A Different Kind of End Times Church

Section 01 - The Roads of Ministry and Business

Chapter 01 – A Different Kind of End Times Church

God has revealed a new mandate for business in the body of Christ. And the biggest confusion that seems to exist right now with regard to this mandate is that people are asking,

"Where does this fit in with the ministry? And if I have a Fivefold Business calling, how does that fit with my ministry calling?"

So in this first section I want to try and explain to you what these two different roads look like. This is so that you can find out which road you are supposed to be on, and how you can approach both ministry and business without any confusion.

A Mystery

The apostle Paul taught that the church was a mystery. In other words the revelation or pattern of the New Testament was not visible in the Old Testament. It wasn't even visible during the ministry of Jesus.

God gave revelation specifically to the apostle Paul, and He gave him a picture of what the New Testament church would look like.

It was very different to what people were expecting. It went right against all Jewish thinking. And for a while I think it blew everybody's minds because it just wasn't what they were expecting. It was so different.

Paul spoke about this mystery and he called it his gospel. In Romans 16:25 and 26 he says,

Now to him that is capable of establishing you according to my gospel, and the preaching of Jesus Christ, according to the revelation of the mystery, which was kept secret since the world began,
But now is being made known, both through the writings of the prophets, and under the instruction of the everlasting God, made known to all nations for the obedience of faith:

And then in Ephesians 3:3 to 5 he says,

How by revelation God made known to me the mystery; (as I wrote before in few words,
Whereby, when you read, you may understand my knowledge in the mystery of Christ)
Which in other ages was not made known to the sons of men, as it is now revealed to his holy apostles and prophets by the Spirit;

So Paul received a specific revelation and he said,

By Les D. Crause

"This revelation is now being revealed to the New Testament apostles and prophets."

It wasn't there before. It builds on what God had before, but it has not been revealed before. It is a mystery.

The End Times Church

There is a new mystery which God is unveiling in this day and age in which we live, and it is mystery of the end times church. You may have read about this plenty of times under the ministry side.

A Glorious Church

What is this mystery? Firstly the church is not going to disappear again like it did in the Dark Ages, to be totally demolished, destroyed and vanish away.

The Lord has been restoring His church, and Jesus is building up His church for His return. And when He comes, He is coming for a glorious and victorious church. This is the message and the mystery of the end times church.

Why is it a mystery? Because if you read all the prophecies in the Old and New Testaments you won't find it.

You will find the story of the anti-Christ, the falling away and everybody turning from the faith. And we have this picture that by the time Jesus returns, the church will almost be non-existent and He will have to come and whip us out quickly before we all die.

That is not what the end times church will look like. So why didn't the Bible tell us?

Because it is a mystery; because God didn't want Satan to know ahead of time what He was going to do. But now in this day and age in which we live, the new mystery of the end times church is being revealed.

A Prosperous Church

What is it that caused the church to go into the Dark Ages? What caused it to die and be destroyed? And what is it today that the church is facing that is causing it to battle to survive and to continue to exist?

It is the power of the world over the church. The church has to be subservient to the world. The world dominates and controls. The World System, under the influence of Lucifer and his cohorts, is set to destroy the church of God.

What power does the world have? It has financial resources. And what power has the church always lacked through the years? It is financial resources.

God has a new plan for the end times church, which will prevent this church from going the same route that the old original church went.

By Les D. Crause

God has a plan to deliver the church from the bondage to the world. That plan is a brand new mandate that involves business.

Right now in this day and age in which we live, God is raising up a new breed of entrepreneurs who carry a Fivefold Business calling, not a Fivefold Ministry calling.

Difference Between Ministry and Business

I want to explain to you the difference between the Fivefold Ministry calling and the Fivefold Business calling, so you can have no doubt in your mind as to exactly what this new business involves.

I want you to be clear what your ministry and your calling will involve if God has called you to such a calling.

Basic Ministry

Let's look at the whole concept of ministry. In Romans 12 we read about all the basic ministries. I have covered this elsewhere and am not going to repeat it here, but there is a series of ministries that are mentioned.

These ministries are actually basic human needs. They are things like the need for encouragement, for leadership, for teaching and instruction, financial help, etc.

These needs can be met either by using spiritual ministry or by financial help. Here they are in Romans 12:5 to 8.

So we, [being] many, are one body in Christ, and every one members of each other.
Having then gifts that vary according to the grace that is given to us, [we should use them], if prophecy, according to the proportion of faith;
If service, in serving: a teacher, in teaching;
If an encourager, in exhortation: one that gives, with generosity; one that rules, with diligence; one that shows compassion, with cheerfulness.

You see these are all basic human needs, and those human needs can be met in a ministry context using ministries that God has given. However they can also be used in a business context by using financial resources that God will give.

Gifts of the Spirit

We look now at gifts of the Spirit. These are not naturalistic. They are totally, 100 percent supernatural, and they come by the empowerment of the Spirit of God.

The spiritual gifts add enabling power to the basic ministries. If you take a basic ministry and add spiritual gifts to it, you bring that basic ministry to a new level and power.

This is because you now add something supernatural to what before could have been purely natural.

By Les D. Crause

This is very easy to see when it comes to ministry. You simply add spiritual gifts to meet these basic needs in a ministry context.

How do you now add supernatural gifts to meet these basic needs in a business or financial context? That is something you need to understand.

Leadership Offices

We have the lower levels of basic ministries. We have the supernatural empowerment of the gifts of the Spirit. And as we put these together they lead upwards into leadership offices.

What is an office? An office is a permanent position not a function. We taught under the Fivefold Ministry that a person who is placed into office is placed permanently in that position.

I taught there that an office is what we are, not what we do. So a prophet in office is somebody who is a prophet, not somebody who prophesies.

Prophetic Office

The fivefold leadership can either be ministry oriented or they can be business oriented. That is new isn't it?

This does not exclude ministry involvements. If you are in the office of a prophet, your Prophetic Ministry is not the same thing.

We have proved again and again, that a person in Prophetic Office is not someone who prophesies, but someone who has authority to decree.

The Prophetic Ministry is something totally different. Somebody in office may function in Prophetic Ministry, but somebody who is not in office can still function in Prophetic Ministry.

Someone who is in a different office like a teaching office, can also still function in Prophetic Ministry because ministry is the lower level. It is a combination of the basic ministries and the gifts of the Spirit which is available to all of us.

Prophetic Entrepreneur

When we come to the business leadership offices, we are now looking at an entrepreneur. And if we look at the example of the prophet again, we are not looking at a ministry Prophetic Office. We are looking at a Prophetic Entrepreneur.

A Prophetic Entrepreneur is not someone who prophesies. You see if you realize that the spiritual office of prophet is not directly linked to the prophetic function, you will understand easier how someone can stand in the Prophetic Office as an entrepreneur, and not be someone who prophesies.

What does a Prophetic Entrepreneur do? He does something very similar to what the spiritual ministry prophet does.

The Prophetic Entrepreneur gives decree concerning business. The ministry prophet gives decree concerning the church and concerning ministries. It is a similar function, but a different direction and a different orientation.

So then can a person who is a Prophetic Entrepreneur function in Prophetic Ministry? Certainly he can, if he is a child of God and has a spiritual ministry. But it is not his office.

You might say to me,

"I'm a Prophetic Entrepreneur, but I feel I should minister to someone prophetically. God has given me revelations and I have a prophetic word.

I want to encourage and motivate and tell people the word from the Lord. Now I can't do it because I'm in business."

No, your ministry office is something totally different to your spiritual ministry. Do not confuse the two.

CHAPTER 02

Ministry Calling Versus Business Calling

Chapter 02 - Ministry Calling Versus Business Calling

What is the ultimate purpose of a ministry calling and a business calling? I am not looking now at ordinary ministries but at leadership offices.

In Ephesians 4, Paul tells us what the prime purpose of the Fivefold Ministry offices of apostle, prophet, evangelist, pastor and teacher are. He says this in Ephesians 4:11 and 12.

And he himself gave some apostles, and some prophets; and some evangelists; and some pastors and teachers; For the equipping of the saints, for the work of the ministry, for the building up of the body of Christ:

Where did Paul speak about the Fivefold Entrepreneurs? Paul didn't speak about it because he did not have the new mystery. He was given the ministry of the early church.

Even though this is a new mystery, I believe Paul's teachings can be used as they are but with a slight variation. I would like to give you the new version as it relates to the Fivefold Business calling.

God has given the leadership ministries, the fivefold business calling, for the equipping of the saints, for the work of business, for the building up of the body of Christ;

It is the same ultimate goal. The only difference is the work of business.

What is the purpose of each of the leadership? On the ministry side it is to provide opportunities for ministry. On the business side it is to provide opportunities for work and business.

On the ministry side it is to provide training for ministry. On the business side it is to provide training for business.

On the ministry side it is to provide leadership for the ministry. These are the leaders in the body of Christ.

On the business side it is to provide leadership for business. These are the leaders who are the business entrepreneurs in the body of Christ.

It is to provide mentorship, protection and covering for both ministry or business, depending on which side and which road you are walking on.

Are you beginning to see the picture? I hope that by the time I am finished you will see the picture very clearly. I hope that you will identify these roads very distinctly, and will know exactly which road you are meant to be walking on.

The Anointing

Let's look now at the anointing of God as we compare ministry versus business. We go down to the lowest level

- the supernatural power of the Holy Spirit manifested in the gifts of the Spirit. Paul tells us in 1 Corinthians 12:4 to 7,

Now there are various different gifts, but the same Spirit.
And there are various different ministries, but the same Lord.
And there are various different [modes of] operation, but it is the same God that operates all [of them] in all [cases].
But the manifestation of the Spirit is given so that everyone can benefit.

Can you see the amount of variations that are possible here?

You say, "Well I have the gift of prophecy, so that means I must be a prophet."

No, there are various different ministries; all the basic ministries that can be involved. And there are various different modes of operation.

You can flow in this revelation, helping somebody to identify ministries. You can flow in the same operation, helping somebody to identify their business capabilities.

There is an anointing which comes from the Holy Spirit. And that anointing can be used either to fulfill the work of the ministry, or it can be used to fulfill the work of business as an entrepreneur.

Differences Between Ministry and Business

What then are the basic differences between these two?

The ministry calling builds church membership. The business calling builds business staff membership.

The ministry calling provides an outlet for people to fulfill their ministries. The business calling provides an outlet for people to work and excel in their business capabilities.

What do we do today? We go to church, get involved and do our ministry.

But when it comes to our secular life, to our daily bread and our work, we have to go and work for an ungodly boss. We have to go into the World System and look to the world to provide our needs.

God is going to change that. It is time that He raises up Christian leaders, entrepreneurs and business owners.

They will provide an environment in which Christians can come and work for a Godly employer, and work towards a goal that benefits the body of Christ.

By Les D. Crause

Similarities Between Ministry and Business

There are also similarities between the two.

Building up the Body

Both of them lead to the building up of the body. Both of them have their prime goal as the building up of the universal church, the body of Christ.

Don't think that because you have a business calling, your calling is to become filthy stinking rich and to go and live a life of luxury. No you don't need a calling to do that. Unbelievers are doing that quite well without the Lord.

You need supernatural empowerment to fulfill this business calling. The central purpose in God giving you this calling is that you are to use it to help build up the body of Christ.

It is for you to fill the gap that has existed all along in the church; the one thing that Satan has power over in the church - financial resources.

Depending on Supernatural Gifts

The second similarity between the two offices is that they both depend on supernatural gifts and abilities. So don't think,

"Well ministry requires an anointing and the supernatural gifts of the Spirit. But business just requires me to go to a good Business School and learn some good worldly business skills. Then I can excel as an entrepreneur."

No, that is not the Fivefold Business calling. The Fivefold Business calling is just as supernatural as the Fivefold Ministry calling.

It will require an empowerment of God on high. It will require a supernatural power from the Holy Spirit in order for you to fulfill this calling.

It is no less supernatural than a ministry calling, so don't say,

"Well he has a Fivefold Ministry calling. I'm just called to go and make money so I can't do anything spiritual anymore. I just have to get into the World System and go and do work, but I wanted to pack up my job to go into the ministry."

Finding the Right Road

How do you find the right road? Which road has God called you to be on?

Has He called you to walk the ministry road, has He called you to walk the business road, or has He called you to walk both roads at the same time?

By Les D. Crause

Let me try and clarify this for you. I think we are going to put all the pieces together now, and perhaps it will begin to make sense. All I want to get across to you in this first section is to help you understand which road you are walking on.

We will continue later on and explain in more detail how each of these Fivefold Business callings function and work; how God will raise them up, and how they will function in the marketplace and in the body of Christ.

Every Believer Has Both

Firstly I want you to see that both ministry and business roles exist in every believer. Everyone has a ministry in the body of Christ, whether they are in leadership or not.

From the day you were born again, you were placed into the body of Christ supernaturally by the Holy Spirit. You became a member, whether it was the small pinkie or the big toe.

Whatever you are, you are a part of the body of Christ, and as such you have a ministry function in the body of Christ.

However we also all have a responsibility to bring in our daily bread. Paul says,

If a man will not work, neither let him eat.

We have a responsibility to go out daily to work, to earn our keep and to provide for our families. Every single believer has a ministry function and a work function. And if you want to find the word business in Scripture you won't find it there.

I did a teaching on this once and it was a little bit imbalanced. This is because I was looking at it purely from a ministry context.

I showed very clearly that the place you will find business in Scripture always relates to work in your secular job.

Every believer has these. Each believer can function in business. They can function well in business and even go into their own business or be a freelancer. They can work for themselves without having a fivefold calling.

In the same way, every believer can have a ministry in the body of Christ without being called to the Fivefold Ministry offices.

Don't confuse these two. Don't think that because you enjoy doing business you now no longer have a ministry.

No, you are a member of the body of Christ. You are a child of God and you will always have a ministry to carry out.

By Les D. Crause

Moving to a Ministry Office

When you move into a ministry office however everything changes. Now it is totally different.

The Fivefold Ministry has always been required to give up their secular work and their business in order to fulfill the call.

Jesus called Peter and John while they were fishing. They were carrying out their secular job which was working in their fishing business. Jesus called them to give up their fishing business and to devote themselves completely to the work of the ministry.

After Jesus died Peter said,

"I'm going back to fishing again because everything is over."

But Jesus came and appeared to him on the beach, and we have that famous passage where He asked three times,

"Peter do you love me?"

Each time He asked Peter that question He gave him a new ministry call, and Peter never did go back to fishing.

No Income for Ministry

When someone is called to a Fivefold Ministry office, they are required to relinquish their career and their business involvement in order to devote themselves entirely to the work of God.

That is where the problem takes place, because suddenly there is no financial income.

Very often you see businessmen or women; entrepreneurs who have functioned well in business. They get the call of God and He calls them to give it all up for the sake of the ministry.

Then they go out and live in poverty because nobody wants to support them. Nobody wants to give to them, because now people think that they are calling for charity.

It has been that way from the beginning and it is still that way today. People are not pouring their financial resources into the body of Christ. And even when business owners do it, they do it with strings attached.

They say, "I the wealthy businessman, will give you, poor little church, a lot of my money so that I can be special. I can control and call the shots and tell you what to do in your church."

By Les D. Crause

He will be on the Board of Directors, and she will be one of the top directors of the church and the elders. And they are there controlling the body of Christ because they are manipulating through money.

This is going to come to an end now, because God is raising up a new Fivefold Ministry office; a Fivefold Ministry office that devotes themselves entirely and completely to the generation of financial wealth.

CHAPTER 03

Ministry and Business Working Together

Chapter 03 – Ministry and Business Working Together

You can have the same thing in reverse. What happens if God has called you to the Fivefold Business calling and you are in ministry?

It works exactly the same as a person who is called to the Fivefold Ministry. You cannot devote yourself fully to the work of God while you are doing a secular job.

You also cannot devote yourself completely to the generation of financial wealth to the body of Christ while you are being involved in ministry. It will tear you apart.

You can only walk one of these roads at a time. But put these two together, and now you have fivefold ministers who are devoting themselves completely to the work of the ministry; to the call of God, to building up the body of Christ, and to reaching out to the nations with the gospel.

They don't ever have to worry about financial resources, because God has raised up a whole new division that stands and works side by side.

They are devoted entirely to the generation of wealth, not for personal gain, but to build and to feed the body of Christ.

It will no longer be businessmen giving their pittance into the church. These businessmen will be church leaders.

They will be Fivefold Entrepreneurs, standing shoulder to shoulder with the Fivefold Ministry offices; both of them together standing as leaders in the body of Christ.

Both of them will function supernaturally under the power and anointing of the Holy Spirit. They will accomplish signs and wonders in the spiritual realm, and signs and wonders in the financial realm using the power of God.

Can you imagine a church that has the supernatural power of God, and the supernatural power to generate finances and to accumulate the wealth of this world? It will be a church that will be unstoppable.

It will be a church that will never again be subject to this World System. In fact the world is going to come and bow to us, because we are going to hold the power, the authority and the financial resources.

Only One at a Time

Can you function in both at the same time? No. Can you function in each of these? Yes, you could function in both the Fivefold Ministry and the Fivefold Entrepreneurship, but you cannot do both at the same time.

By Les D. Crause

God may for a season have called you to the Fivefold Ministry. And for a season God may use you in that ministry.

But when the time comes that He calls you to move out into the Fivefold Entrepreneurship, you will have to let go of your Fivefold Ministry office.

You don't let go of your ministry, because your ministry is your function in the body of Christ. You let go of your office not your function. Can you see that clearly?

You are going to take an office as a leader in the body of Christ; a leader in the financial realm as a Fivefold Entrepreneurs.

We will be looking in future teachings at exactly how these Fivefold Entrepreneurs function. We will see what they look like, and how they use the supernatural power of God to function in the body of Christ.

Find Out Where You Stand

Right now where do you stand? Are you just an ordinary church member? Then you have a ministry and you have a job. Be faithful in both of those.

A lot of people want to give up their job and blame the call of the ministry for it.

You say, "You know I can't stand working for my boss. I wish I could just spend all day praying, reading the

Scriptures and ministering to people. Wouldn't that be wonderful? I think God has called me to the Fivefold Ministry."

No, not unless you have been called to one of the fivefold offices of evangelist, pastor, teacher, prophet or apostle.

If you have been called to one of those offices, yes the time will come when you will need to let go of your secular responsibility. Then you will be able to devote yourself fully to the call of God.

But if God has called you to the business side, the same thing is going to apply. You will have to let go of your ministry office.

You might say, "But I'm the pastor of the church."

Give up your church and hand it over to someone else. Then get out there and accumulate the finance to build that church up to become one of the most powerful in the community.

You might say, "But I'll lose my authority. I'll lose my ministry."

No you won't lose your gifts or your ministry abilities. You will continue to do what you do, but you will no longer be what you were. You will now be something else, because a ministry office is who you are.

By Les D. Crause

Can you see the difference? Your whole focus and attention is now going to be on this new thing.

Have you risen up in business and been a highly successful entrepreneur? Have you built up a good financial resource and wealth and have a whole structure set up?

God may be calling you to give it all up for the sake of the call to the Fivefold Ministry. He may want you to let go of your business and devote yourself full time to the work of the ministry.

You see we have always taught that and seen that. It is very easy for us to say,

"Well give up your whole reliance on the natural. Give up your worldly call to take up the spiritual call."

But how difficult it is if you have been in that ministry call, to realize that now suddenly God is pulling you out of it and He's calling you to what looks like a secular call.

It is not a secular call though. It is just as supernatural and just as authoritative and powerful as the call to the ministry.

My Personal Experience

How do I know these things? I have been there and done that.

I have risen to the pinnacle of what is available in the Fivefold Ministry and have functioned in all five of the Fivefold Ministry.

I have risen up to not only be an apostle, but to be an apostolic father, to establish training mechanisms and to train the Fivefold Ministry.

But what is the one thing that has stood in the way all along? It is lack of financial resources.

All the time I want to get involved in the work of the ministry, I have to let go in order to raise enough money to pay the bills. I cannot function that way until God provides a resource that I will never ever have to worry about money again.

How is He going to provide that? By raising up the Fivefold Business entrepreneurs. So God has called me now to step out of my Apostolic Ministry office.

So am I no longer an apostle? No, I just became a different kind of apostle. Am I no longer a prophet? No, I just became a different kind of prophet. Did I lose my gifts of the spirit? No, they function like they always did.

The only difference is I get revelation in different directions now. Instead of praying over people and telling them what ministry calling they have, I tell them what business calling they have.

By Les D. Crause

We are going to build something that has never existed before in the body of Christ. We are going to build a financial resource that is going to be part and parcel of this new move.

The Solomon Era

This is what the Solomon era is all about. God raised up Solomon in times past to bring wealth and prosperity in Israel.

In the same way, God in this day and age is raising up the Solomon apostle, to bring the church to a place of prosperity and glory and financial resources that have never been known before.

Do you feel that fire burning in you? Do you desire to see the church of God rise up and conquer and take this world? If you do then maybe you have been trying to fulfill that vision up until now in a ministry calling.

You can still fulfill that same vision, that same fire and passion and burden. It doesn't change. All that changes is your focus.

Instead of now getting out there and trying to do it yourself, you are going to raise up the resources that will send the Fivefold Ministry throughout the world.

They will turn this world upside down. They will transform the church and bring the body of Christ to the place that God has called it to be.

Together we will go forward in power and overcome this world. The world will bow to us. Instead of going to the world to beg for finances, the world will be coming to us and saying,

"How did you do it? How are you raising all this money? What secrets do you have?"

We will say, "Well we have one main secret. His name is Jesus. Come on in and we'll show you a bit more."

What a power we are going to have! Instead the church is going and saying,

"Well you know we have the Lord. We don't need money."

And you wonder why the church went into the Dark Ages. It is not going to happen again.

By God's grace this new mandate is going to transform the body of Christ around the world. It is going to bring us to that place where we will finally turn this world upside down for the Lord. Then the church will be ready for Jesus to come and take us to Himself.

By Les D. Crause

Section 02 - The Preparation of an Entrepreneur

CHAPTER 04

Preparation in the Work Place

Section 02 - The Preparation of an Entrepreneur

Chapter 04 – Preparation in the Work Place

Some time back when God first gave me this mandate for business, I did a teaching called Signs of the Fivefold Business Calling. That was a kind of introduction to this whole concept of being an entrepreneur for the Lord.

I want to continue now in the vein of what is involved in becoming God's entrepreneur. So in this section I want to look at the preparation that God puts a person through when He has called them to this level of calling.

It can be very confusing when you compare ministry and business, but they actually work very well together.

In the ministry realm we had the Fivefold Ministry and we saw the various levels of apostle, prophet, evangelist, pastor and teacher. The greatest leadership ministry of course was the apostle.

And so we looked at the apostle and saw that there were different kinds of apostle. We saw that an apostle is somebody who rises up, gets trained in all the ministries, and is able to function in virtually everything.

It is interesting that at the time when I taught on the apostolic preparation, I used an illustration to try and help you understand how God trains His apostles.

The illustration I used was business. If you have gone through this teaching you will see that I was talking about business right back there already.

Many of the principles that I will be sharing here on the preparation of an apostolic entrepreneur are very much the same as the apostolic preparation, but they are slightly different.

So if you want a full picture, go and review the apostolic preparation because I'm not going to repeat what I taught there. But if you put the two together you are going to have a full picture.

This is because the chances are if God has called you to be His entrepreneur, He has already called you to the apostolic level of ministry as well. You can find what I shared in my book entitled The Apostolic Calling.

Much More Than a Businessman

The Apostolic Ministry and the entrepreneur kind of run side by side.

What exactly is an entrepreneur? An entrepreneur, according to the world, is simply someone who has started, owns and runs a business.

By Les D. Crause

An entrepreneur is far more than that though. I would like to take this term and use it in place of the ministry of the apostle. So when we speak about the apostle, we are speaking about the ministry leadership.

When we speak about an entrepreneur, we are speaking about the business leadership. So if you like, the entrepreneur is God's apostle to the business realm.

Functions in All Business Areas

The entrepreneur needs to be a Jack of all trades. Just like the apostle needs to be one who functions in all ministries, the entrepreneur should be one who can function in all types of business activity.

The entrepreneur should be someone who has worked his way up through the ranks.

That is the illustration I used in the apostolic preparation. I described somebody who starts at the lowest level and works their way up until they become the Managing Director of the company and reach the highest level.

The entrepreneur must be a captain who has learned to sail all types of business boats. We considered this in the series The God Kind of Business.

So I want to first look at how God prepares the entrepreneur. Then after that we will look in a bit more detail at the kind of training that the entrepreneur goes through.

When you compare it again with the apostle, the entrepreneur needs to be able to function in many different kinds of jobs and in many different kinds of businesses. The entrepreneur should also be able to relate to many different niches or groups.

My Personal Experiences

I would like to look in a bit more detail at some of these. And to help to illustrate it, I am going to take myself once again as an example.

I know that God has called me to this level of leadership and function as His entrepreneur. And so I am hoping that some of the experiences that I have had along the way are going to be similar experiences to what you have gone through.

It is not going to be the same. God prepares and trains each of us differently, according to our background, according to where we were born and lived, and many different things in our lives. So I don't expect you to say,

"Well I didn't go through those experiences. Maybe I'm not an entrepreneur."

I just want you to see what you can identify with in some of the things that I share. And perhaps you will see some similar patterns in the way God has prepared you for this calling.

Let's look first then at God's preparation in different kinds of jobs, at all different employee levels.

Working As a Casual Employee

The very first job that I had was as a casual employee. It is what they called them in those days.

I was still a young guy. I don't think I was even a teenager yet. If I was I may have just turned into a teenager, but I think I was probably 11 years old or something. It was so far back I can't remember.

My mother worked for a clothing company that was like an outfitters. That was her regular job.

During the school holidays they would take in casual employees to come and work part time and earn a bit of extra pocket money. So naturally with my mother working there I got the chance to get in there and do my very first job.

Well I always did work around the house but I was never paid for it. This was the first time I was doing any work where I would actually get paid for it.

I remember walking in there and they said,

"Okay, what you need to do is to be there to help all the customers. You must help them if they are having a problem and show them things. Just be there for whatever they need."

So they put me out there and I think it was a Saturday morning. They were having a special sale and the place was crowded with people.

What was my job? It was to make people buy. Well you know I had never been trained for this kind of thing before. All I needed to do was to go and help, and I was as helpful as I could be.

I was there watching people when they picked up the clothes, and I would be there to say,

"Can I help you? Are you looking for another color?"

I just did whatever I could. I never stood still for a moment. I walked round and round the shop looking for people that needed help. I wanted to really impress them, to get a good reputation in this job.

Afterwards one of my mother's bosses said to her,

"Who was that young guy we had here today? He was really amazing the way he walked round and round. Whenever the customers had a need he was there. I was really impressed with him."

She said, "That was my son!"

By Les D. Crause

I felt so good. It was my first job and I excelled in it. And it was so wonderful to finally get the measly little money they gave you, but it was my own money that I had earned.

You see that was the lowest level of employee you can get, and that was where I started.

If you ever want to move into this business calling, you will need to have some exposure to working in the business realm. And so the lowest level is starting as a casual or temporary worker, or a plain ordinary employee.

Working for the Post Office

After I left school my exposures were to all the big corporations and Government organization type jobs. Here you were such a tiny little cog in the machine that if you were to disappear nobody would notice.

My very first job was one which I took on, simply because I didn't have money to go to University which I was hoping to do. I thought I would get a job at the Post Office, which was a Government owned corporation.

They had the Telecommunications Division. Here they would train you how to look after the whole telephone system, and to go and work in all the different divisions in telecommunications.

There was a hope that if I went through their training course and showed potential, that they would then send me to university to study the thing that I really wanted - Electrical Engineering.

I really wanted to be an electrical engineer, but nobody wanted to pay money for me to go and study it. I never had the money and my folks couldn't afford to send me. So I got this job hoping that if I went on their training course I would rise up.

I found out that not only was I a small cog in the machine, but there were a lot of other cogs that looked a lot better than me.

They stood a far better chance of going to University than I did, and they were not going to send everybody. They were going to select one or two and that was it.

It didn't take me long to realize that I did not have what it took to rise up and be that big engineer that everyone would look up to. I was just relegated to ordinary employee or non-entity in a very big company.

Well there was no point in continuing this training course because I was far more intelligent than the people I was being trained with. Most of them had left with lower school qualifications than me, and I had only taken this job in the hope of going to university.

So if I wasn't going to go to university I could get a better job than that. I had the highest qualifications you could

By Les D. Crause

have in school at that time. I was highly qualified, or so I thought. But all I was qualified in was intellect. I didn't know how to do the job.

Working for the Railways

I left that job and joined another big organization called the Railways; you know the people who operate the trains. It was a huge organization and they had a job going in the scientific realm.

Well I was scientific. I had a scientific mind. They didn't have anything going in electrical engineering, but I chose the next best thing: Laboratory Assistant.

Again I thought the same thing. I thought I could get in there and really impress these people. I could work hard and work my way up. It was a big organization and I thought,

"Maybe I can rise up and go on one of their training courses. I can go and get a degree and become somebody important."

I remember the first day I walked into the job in the Laboratory. I had such zeal and I let everyone know what great things I was going to accomplish; how big I was going to become, how hard I was going to study, and how perfect I was going to become.

The guys who worked there tolerated me for a bit. Then they called me aside and said,

Preparation in the Work Place

"Les, you're working for the Railways now. Calm down, just do your job and get paid. Enjoy the weekends and your annual vacation and everything will go fine because you are going nowhere."

Well that burst my bubble. I thought,

"I'll work for a bit and save money and go to university."

It took a while for me to realize they were right. There was no point in rocking the boat. Just be an ordinary employee, do your job well, don't rock the boat and get your pay each month.

Every year they gave you an annual increase. Your pay went up a little bit and you just continued to do this highly technical job.

The main job I had at that time was to take some of the oils that they drained from the diesel engines. You put it into a little pot, stuck it on a heater with a flame over it and waited for it to go 'bah'.

When it went 'bah' you measured the temperature. That was it. It was known as calculating the flash point.

That was my main job. Every now and then they gave me something different to test.

The really good chemical tests and things were for the senior guys. I was just a little dog's body nobody.

By Les D. Crause

Eventually they gave me more technical jobs, but really I was just a Laboratory Assistant.

Well my great big aspirations for rising up, having a career and being somebody high up in business began to die more and more.

Then I went through a season where suddenly God called me to the ministry.

I thought, "Well that's why I never succeeded in business, because God had called me to the ministry. That was obviously the case."

Working for an Aircraft Company

Off we went into ministry and I failed in ministry too. Then I went back to work. This time I went to work again for another Government owned corporation. It was an aircraft company.

At that time we had moved from Rhodesia where I had grown up down to South Africa. Now here I was in this famous job just being an ordinary admin clerk.

I had to get up early in the morning, get on the bus to travel to a nearby city where the job actually was. And there I was, annexed to the Air Force.

I wasn't in the military. I was just working as a civilian, but it was with all Air Force personnel. There I was doing my famous little admin job, coming home at night and getting paid an absolute pittance.

Those were my experiences at being an ordinary casual employee.

By Les D. Crause

CHAPTER 05

Rising Up in the Work Place

Chapter 05 – Rising Up in the Work Place

You might say to me,

"If God has called me to great things, why should I have to go through those ordinary jobs and be an ordinary nobody?"

Because one day you are going to employ ordinary little nobodies, and you had better understand that person's position.

You need to understand their aspirations, their frustrations and what they are going through. You have to start at the bottom and work your way up.

When you are ready, God will open up the way for you to move up a notch or two. But you must be faithful. The Scripture says,

Be faithful in that which is least and you will be faithful in much.

The same thing applies in your business. If you haven't learned to be faithful as an ordinary little employee, how can you be trusted to move higher?

And if God can't trust you to be an ordinary little employee for Him, how can He trust you to be His entrepreneur? Be faithful with what God has given you.

Stay where you are and God will promote you and lift you up when the time is right.

I had my chance eventually. I packed up my job in the Laboratory, in the hope that I could spend a bit of time at Bible School.

My wife was going to carry on working, so I packed up my job. But straight after that she fell pregnant and had to give up her job. Now we were in trouble.

Back to the Railways

Living with my parents was another story. It was preparation time, but that was more like prophetic preparation, so I won't go into that.

But the time came where I went back to work again, and guess where it was? It was for the Railways - but not in the Laboratory this time.

I got a new job in the Personnel Division handling pay and personnel records. I was given the job of taking a particular kind of railway staff. In my case I was dealing with all the running staff - the guys who actually ran the trains.

I remember the very first section that I had was to deal with all the train guards. It was one of the ranks on the trains.

By Les D. Crause

The guard is the guy who stands right at the back. He waves the flag and directs everything from the back of the train.

So the guards were my section, and I did the pay for all the guards and whatever personnel records needed to be kept. Whatever personnel information needed to be maintained for these people was my responsibility.

The wonderful thing about that job was that I had a boss who liked me. I think the reason he liked me was because it turned out that I went to the same school as his children.

Then he found out that I had had this very good education at school and he was really impressed with education. He said to me,

"You should be working in a far better position than you are now."

Well I kind of knew that from when I was in the Laboratory already. One of my bosses there said to me,

"You're an idiot working here! With the kind of intelligence you have I'm going to have you fired, just so you can go and get a better job."

It isn't often that a boss tells you that, but he wasn't the main boss. He was the sub-boss and he didn't care. But now here I was and there was someone who recognized my potential.

He said, "I want you to write a letter to the big bosses and say that in view of your great educational qualifications you feel you should be earning a lot more. I'll also add my recommendation."

After this I got an unexpected pay increase. It was amazing.

Acting the Boss

Then the next moment my boss went on vacation. The arrangement was that when he went on vacation, one of the staff below him had to rise up into his position and become the supervisor.

The wonderful thing was when you become supervisor they paid you his salary while you were acting in his place. Well I wasn't very high on the lower grades, so jumping from my salary to his almost doubled my pay.

Here I was now and I was one of the ordinary Joe's in this big office. He was the corner office guy; the boss. And he was saying that he wanted me to act as supervisor in his place when he went on leave.

Well how do you suppose the rest of the people in that office felt about that?

I wasn't one of the main guys there at all. I was just a little Johnny come lately. A lot of them had been there

By Les D. Crause

for years already, but here I was stepping into the corner office.

They were coming to me and asking,

"Is it all right if I go home early today? I have a doctor's appointment at 2:00 o'clock today. Is it okay if I go?"

I said, "Yes sure."

"I need some help with this. Can you help me here?"

"Yes sure."

It was a wonderful feeling to finally rise up and be supervisor. And I found an amazing thing being a supervisor. When I was just one of the ordinary employees, I would always go to my boss to clear something with him in case I did it wrong. I would say,

"Is it all right if I do it this way or should I do it that way? What do you think I should do here?"

I always felt that I needed to get his permission or his go-ahead before I did something. But now suddenly people were coming to me and asking me the same things, and I had to make the decision.

It was a strange experience at first, but I suddenly realized,

"You know what? I **can** make a decision. I do know what to do in that situation. I do have a recommendation that I believe is the best thing a person can do in a situation."

I realized that a lot of the time I was going to my boss to ask him things that I could actually have answered myself. It was all just a mindset.

When you are put into a position of supervisor and carry the responsibility of actually making decisions and taking responsibility for those decisions, it does something inside of you. It takes you up to a whole new level.

And so my little experience there in the Personnel Division took me to a new level of authority that I didn't realize I had.

Customer Support and Programming

Later on I ended up in a job finally doing the things I loved to do. This was computer programming and customer support. I had a Christian boss and it was just the two of us working in the office.

Well I was just an employee, but we were kind of like partners and we had a close relationship. We fellowshipped in the Lord, and although I wasn't a supervisor, I was at a level where I could make decisions that were very important to the company.

By Les D. Crause

I had the opportunity to work at a level where I was kind of more than a supervisor. I was working more like a director of the company.

Later on the Lord gave me another job just like that, also in the computer side, where I worked almost as a partner.

In fact people would often think that I was the partner in the company to my boss, because sometimes I knew more than he did. Often I knew more than him, but we each had our different roles.

Yes people knew that he owned the company. But they thought we were partners because I carried a level of responsibility in that company.

I had come to the place now where I wasn't just an ordinary employee. I was somebody who was important to the company.

I wasn't just a small cog that could disappear. I was one of the main cogs. And if you took that cog out the machine would battle to function. I was starting to become important.

CHAPTER 06

Standing On My Own in Business

Chapter 06 – Standing On My Own in Business

After this experience it was time to learn what it was like to stand on my own. The next area of training was to be a freelancer.

What is a freelancer? A freelancer is a person who works for themselves. You are not working for an organization and you are not working under a boss. You are working for yourself.

You are doing the work and getting all the pay for it. You are in charge. You are the supervisor, the employer, the employee - you're everything.

That is kind of a hybrid that takes you from being an ordinary employee up to the higher level that we are aiming for.

Life Assurance

My first opportunity to do that came in the Life Assurance realm. I was battling financially, wondering how we could ever rise up higher, and someone came to try and sell me life assurance. I couldn't afford to buy, but he said to me,

"Why don't you try selling life assurance?"

I said, "I don't even know if I can sell. I've never really tried."

So I went for my interviews. They tested me and tried me and were foolish enough to employ me. And there I was. I was kind of working for a company, but I was only being paid commissions on what I sold.

I was in my own business. And even though I was working under their banner, it was my first transition from being under a company to doing my own thing. It was kind of a mixture between the two.

I had to schedule my own time and make my own appointments. They gave me an office to work in and that was the only time they saw me there.

Once a week we had a sales meeting where we would meet with all the other sales reps. That was my sole involvement with the company, apart from the pay check that I got from them.

Other than that I was on my own. I was a freelancer, and if I didn't work I didn't eat.

Multi-Level Marketing

The Life Assurance selling became a bit too much. I couldn't keep it up and I tried something different. These days they call it MLM or Multi-Level Marketing.

By Les D. Crause

I don't even remember how it happened, but someone invited us to come to a meeting where we were told that we could make a lot of money. So we went to this meeting, and everybody there was enthusiastic, keen and excited.

They demonstrated their products and they had some awesome detergent. They took a piece of carpet and rubbed crayon all over it. They dropped ink on it and put all sorts of muck on it, and it was filthy dirty. Then they said,

"Now just look at what our product can do."

They sprayed a couple of times and then put their finger on it and the carpet was clean. Wow, what awesome stuff! Everybody was so enthusiastic and excited.

They had a whole lot of other products as well. There was a range of detergents, jewelry and health care products.

Then they told me what kind of money I could earn if I sold their products. If I not only sold their products, but if I could find other people to sell the products, I would get commission on what everyone else sold.

You would build up this whole pyramid, where people under you were those you had introduced. They then introduced other people who introduced other people.

They all came under you and all of their sales added a little bit. Eventually you could just sit back and do nothing and all the money would come in all the time. At least that's how it sounded. It sounded too good to be true.

They said, "If you sold just one bottle every day you could make this kind of money. If you brought in so many new agents you could make so much money."

My eyes were boggling at the figures and I thought,

"I don't have to work so hard anymore. I can just set this thing up and the money will roll in."

That is the deception of MLM. It is still going today.

Why did the Lord take me out of what I was doing and put me into MLM? Because MLM is a very big business opportunity out there today and it is a way of selling.

It is a form of direct selling where you do not have to advertise. You don't have companies selling your product. You only sell directly through agents and you get very high commissions.

It costs very little for your product and you sell it at a very high price. And between the cost price and the selling price, there are about 30 or 40 people that are each paid something out of it.

By Les D. Crause

Spreads Like a Cancer

It is a very clever form of advertising and it just spreads like a cancer into the marketplace, because everybody knows somebody who knows somebody else.

The whole idea is that you find the people that you know and get them to see the people they know. They in turn see other people that they know.

As you get all of these circles of influence together everybody gets in. And in the end you don't need to even sell any of the products to the end user.

At the end of the day most of the people who bought it were people who were buying it to sell it.

I would buy it and I would sell it to the people who were going to resell it to other people. Those people were also going to resell it. In the end I don't know if anybody actually used it.

It was a great product. I loved it. Even today I love those products. In fact they did such a good sell job on me that I would still try and sell the product, it was so good.

MLM is a brilliant marketing system. But you know at the end of the day you still have to sell. You still have to make the sales calls and you still have to see the people. You have to be prepared to make the effort to get out there.

It sounds great. If you could just get so many people to sell for you, you could sit and do nothing. Yes, but do you know how much effort it takes to get people to sell for you?

And then once you have people like that you have to keep them selling for you, because the people you bring in are just like you. They are looking forward to getting to the place where they can sit back and do nothing.

It's easy to say,

"If you just sold one bottle a day..."

Heck, I battled to sell one bottle a week; sometimes one bottle a month. It was heavy going. Once you run out of friends and contacts, who do you sell to? I was not going to go and knock on doors and sell it to strangers. I was not going to say,

"Hello, I'd like to offer you this detergent. It normally cost about $2 in the shops, but our one costs $20. How would you like one?"

Who is going to buy it?

You had to invite people to these parties. I remember my turn came one day to stand up and be the demonstrator at one of these parties. And you know they always told the same jokes, and everybody laughed at the jokes that you have told 100 times.

By Les D. Crause

The newcomer comes in and thinks,

"Hey this guy's really funny. Everyone is laughing at his jokes."

That joke was so canned it just wasn't true. But there is an atmosphere that gets created. That is MLM selling. It is a very relevant kind of selling. God was giving me experience in all these different kinds of businesses.

Programming at Last

And then I got the opportunity to get into the thing I've always wanted to do: play with computers and program.

These were all my freelance jobs. The time came when I was eventually charging people per hour for the programs that I was writing.

Well that was a whole lot better than selling a bottle of detergent for $10 and making just two or three dollars out of it. Now I was charging them $50 an hour and writing programs that took me 8 to 10 hours.

That was a whole lot better. I went up a notch. But you know what? I still had to find people to sell to.

That is the problem with freelancing. Freelancing is great. But the problem is you have to be the director, the admin clerk and the sales rep. You have to be the product manager. You have to be everything.

It's a great exposure and experience at a lower level. But I don't care how much you are charging per hour, there are only 24 hours in a day. And some of those hours you have to spend sleeping or eating.

Some of them you have to spend in the bathroom. And others you just have to spend resting, doing nothing, socializing or traveling to work.

By the time you add up the number of hours you have left, even if you can put in an 18 hour day which is really pushing it, if you're charging $100 an hour, that gives you $1 800 a day.

That might be a pretty good income, but you will never become a millionaire that way. You will never rise up to that higher level to be God's entrepreneur if you just stay as a freelancer.

So I had my time as a freelancer, but you have to move a bit higher now. You have to become a business owner. You need to expand and get people working with you and under you.

My Own Computer Business

And so I stepped out to start my own computer business. Not only were we going to offer programming, but we would sell the materials.

By Les D. Crause

We would sell computers as well as the accessories - in fact everything related to computers. Then we would write our programs and resell them.

We were moving to a whole new level. I could bring other people in to work with me. It was awesome to have the liberty and freedom to say,

"I have a computer business and it has a name."

However there was suddenly now all the paperwork that goes with it. We had to rent an office so there were some new expenses as well.

Also if you are employing someone else, you have to try and make enough money to pay them as well. It is a whole new ballpark.

Looking back, I could not have jumped from casual employee to business owner could I? You see I had to work my way through the ranks. So exposure to each level is absolutely necessary before you are ready.

So I had my computer business and we kind of made it through by the skin of our teeth. We had just enough money to pay the rent and just enough money to pay for food.

It was wonderful to be my own boss, but if I didn't work 18 hours a day we didn't eat. You know when you are working for a boss you go home when work is over. You can watch TV all night or do whatever you like.

You come back to work at starting time in the morning. You don't lie awake at night wondering whether your boss is going to have enough money to pay you your salary. It is his problem, not yours.

Well you learned a little bit of that when you went into the freelancer side, but now it takes on a whole new dimension.

Now you are lying awake at night wondering where you are going to get the money to pay the people under you, or enough money to pay the rent for the business.

You are carrying that whole load and that care. It takes a while before you are ready to face that, and you need to be in that experience to feel the pressure that comes on you.

If you have never been there you cannot rise up and lead others. You also cannot be the kind of leader that God has called you to be.

You cannot rise up and get the wealth of this world to come in to supply the body of Christ; to change the world and to get the church ready for the Bridegroom.

That is the ultimate call for God's entrepreneur isn't it? I shared that in the Signs of the Business Calling?

By Les D. Crause

Start of a Training School

The Lord delivered me from the computer business and took me overseas to where I could then start doing another kind of business I had never ever done before. This time it was to set up an online training school.

That was awesome. There were different people involved. We started with a small team and eventually grew bigger and bigger, until we had lecturers who were handling it.

We set up an online bookshop where we could start producing our own books, tapes, DVDs and CDs and all sorts of things on the Internet. We moved up to a whole new level.

These were all the different kinds of jobs that God took me through before He could get me to that place where He said,

"Okay now you step fully into the place that I have called you to be, as my entrepreneur to the nations and to the body of Christ."

Now you may not have gone through that many different and varied jobs.

But if God has called you to this kind of calling, I'll guarantee that as you look at your work history and the experiences you have had along the way, you have had a varied exposure to jobs. This has dealt with various things in you and has prepared you to rise up and be trained.

You must remember that the preparation is not the training. The preparation is to make you ready to be trained. We will deal with training in the next section.

In this section we are looking only at the preparation to become an entrepreneur. God will prepare you in all different kinds of businesses.

CHAPTER 07

Preparation of Fivefold Entrepreneurs

Chapter 07 - Preparation of Fivefold Entrepreneurs

I have already shared a bit about where I have been. I am going to go back over it again from a different viewpoint now and show you the different kinds of businesses.

You see God prepares His apostle to function in different kinds of ministries. We have seen that the apostle will function in the evangelistic, pastoral, teaching and prophetic ministries, before he or she can rise up and take that office of the apostle.

Before you can take the office of entrepreneur in God's economy, you will need to go through different kinds of businesses that are actually closely related to those ministries of evangelist, pastor, teacher and prophet.

So as I look back again on some of the exposures that I had, I can see why I had such varied job opportunities and exposures to different kinds of work. It was in order to prepare me to function in each of these entrepreneurial types.

Evangelistic Entrepreneur

The Evangelistic Entrepreneur is involved in selling and setting up a business. It is just like an evangelist in ministry is involved in selling the gospel and starting churches.

MLM

My little exposure to MLM was my first look at what is involved in setting up a business.

It wasn't really a business, but they call it having your own business. The whole idea is you find a couple of people to work under you and you introduce them.

The moment you do that you move to a level higher. You then receive commissions from their selling. They in turn bring other people in, which makes them move higher and it pushes you higher still.

You get this pyramid structure, but in the end everybody under you in your pyramid is part of your business. And although you are selling somebody else's product it is still your business. You are earning the commission from all those different sales.

So MLM was my first exposure to what it would be like to start from nowhere and begin to build up a business structure.

Life Assurance

Life Assurance was my next exposure. In Life Assurance, again it is your own business.

Some of the people I was working with were making so much money that they were hiring their own secretaries to contact their customers and to set up appointments.

By Les D. Crause

Even though they had an office by the company, they were setting up their own equipment and computer management systems.

They had their own secretary and staff or whoever they wanted to hire. They were running their own businesses.

It was good exposure for me to see how I should think as a person who owns his own business, where I am responsible for my business. And let's face it, if you don't sell you do not have a business.

If an evangelist doesn't preach the gospel he cannot start churches.

I was exposed to situations where selling was the key to building your business. And as you sold effectively you began to bring together a structure which would become a business environment.

Waterproofing Roofs

The Lord then threw me into something that was totally out of my league. I ended up getting a job with a company that sold waterproofing for roofs.

The owner was a Christian man who was prepared to offer me a job and it was a golden opportunity for me. I had no choice but to take it.

But here I was. I had a lot of experience in many things, but buildings and waterproofing was not one of them. I was what was called a 'pen pusher' in those days.

I was really good with my pen - good at writing and even good at speaking. But climbing on roofs and waterproofing them against leakage from rain was not one of my specialties.

I knew nothing about it. But I needed exposure to all different realms of business, and I needed to learn to get in there.

So after a very short bit of training I was climbing on roofs and pretending I really knew what I was doing. I was convincing customers to spend a lot of money to put an expensive waterproofing system on their roofs.

It was a new kind of selling that I had never done before. But I realized that you need to be able to sell to every different kind of person. I was getting exposure to a more varied type of market.

If you are to rise up and be God's entrepreneur, like the apostle you should be able to do anything. So you should be able to get involved in any kind of business.

You say, "Well you know my specialty is the engineering business."

Or you say, "It's this particular type of product in business that I am really good at."

By Les D. Crause

Well if God has called you to be His entrepreneur, get ready for change. He is going to put you into something you know nothing about. It is part of your preparation.

When it all goes wrong; when the business you've been doing suddenly falls apart and you are forced now to go and do something you have never done before and don't feel confident in, don't moan and groan and say,

"The devil has really destroyed my work."

No, God is preparing you for a higher calling.

You might say, "I really don't like selling."

If you want to be God's entrepreneur, you had better know how to be an Evangelistic Entrepreneur, because it is the foundation and the key to all business.

You say, "Well I'll employ other people to do the selling."

How will you know if they are doing it right unless you've been there? How will you know what problems they are facing, unless you have been there? It is part of your preparation. You cannot avoid it.

Pastoral Entrepreneur

Next I had to learn to be the Pastoral Entrepreneur, and that was great.

Teaching Software

My first job in computers actually wasn't a programming job at all. When the company sold a computer, my job was to go in afterwards and teach people how to use the computer.

There was a package of free software that came with every computer that they bought. So my job was to go afterwards to visit them, to teach them how to use the software, and to handle all the problems that they had.

Programming and Support

Can you see the pastoral thing - caring for people and helping them? My next job after this was the same. It just went to a higher level. It was programming and customer support.

It was wonderful to be the nice guy; to walk into a company with a whole big office of women sitting on their computers. You walked in the door and they said,

"There he is! Les we're so glad you're here. We have problems. Please come and help us."

It felt so good to walk in there and to sort their problems out for them. And I tell you they loved me.

Well maybe they didn't love me. They loved who I was and what I was doing. But that was okay. You see I had the pastoral heart and I wanted to help people.

By Les D. Crause

I loved helping people. I thrived on it. They would invite me to their Christmas parties because they loved me so much. It was good pastoral training. I really enjoyed it and it was awesome.

Finally I got to work with people who were not saying,

"No I don't want to buy this. Stop trying to push me to buy your product."

It was tough being in evangelistic preparation, but the pastoral preparation was wonderful. I was there to help people. They were more than willing to receive my help and they cried out for it.

If only we could just stay in that realm forever. But there's a bit more involved to being an entrepreneur than being the nice guy.

Teaching Entrepreneur

There was another nice thing that I also enjoyed because it was also part of my strength. That was being a Teaching Entrepreneur or someone who imparts knowledge.

Teaching Computers and Software

It was great when I began to train people how to use their computers and the software. I could spend time all day, sitting learning the software and all the things that were involved with it, then going out and teaching people how to use it.

That was great. I enjoyed using my knowledge. I could accumulate knowledge, go on a learning phase and get paid for it.

It was part of my job to learn new things and to teach them to others. It is wonderful if you have that same teaching orientation.

If you don't have a teaching orientation you are not going to enjoy this, but you will have to go through it. Because you see teaching others and imparting knowledge to them it is part of being an entrepreneur.

It may be your weakness, and you can't understand why you have been forced into a job giving technical support, when you know nothing about the technical side of things. But it is necessary because you have to be an all-round entrepreneur.

Sharing My Knowledge

The Lord gave me the opportunity to get into online marketing. And guess what I was doing? I was selling my education. I was selling my knowledge.

I didn't plan to do this but I was forced into it. We were starving. There was no money, and the source of income that I had coming in every month without me having to do anything suddenly dried up.

By Les D. Crause

Now I had to find some way of making money in a foreign land with no source of income. So we went for a walk on the beach one day and I said,

"The only thing I can see for us to do is to preach into camera, record the tapes, and then see if we can sell the tapes and get an income."

Knowledge is one of the best products out there. And you know because of that I developed an entire training system for the whole of the Fivefold Ministry, for the apostles and the prophets. And now by God's grace I am doing the same for His entrepreneurs.

We have a whole business going of selling information. Well I could never have done that if I had never become the Teaching Entrepreneur could I?

Teaching is one of the more powerful aspects of being an entrepreneur. You would be amazed at what knowledge you have that you can impart and that people are prepared to pay for.

Prophetic Entrepreneur

Then came the more spiritual part which took a little more than just hard work and knowledge. It required revelation.

You see the Evangelistic Entrepreneur sells and sets up businesses. The Pastoral Entrepreneur helps employees and customers, and the Teaching Entrepreneur educates people.

But then we come to the one who directs and motivates employees and customers. This is the Prophetic Entrepreneur.

It was great offering our training as a business and a product to sell, and to have people pay us to be trained as prophets.

We would sell them a beautiful pack with something like 25 tapes and printed books in it. We thought,

"This is wonderful. People will buy these. They will read the books and listen to the tapes and become prophets."

The trouble was they didn't. In fact they didn't even listen to the tapes. They wanted to be spoon fed. They wanted us to take them and mold them.

Developing Revelation

Well how are you going to do that on the Internet when you haven't even met these people face to face? You do it only one way: by revelation.

I first developed my prophetic ability by marrying a woman who never told me what was going on in her mind. I had to play 20 questions to try and guess what it was that I did wrong because she didn't talk. I would say to her,

"Is it this? Is it that? Was it that?"

Eventually I started to get revelation and I would say,

"Aha, I know what it is. That's your problem."

She would react and I would say,

"Yup, I got it."

My prophetic preparation is another story which I have told elsewhere, but we had this kind of thing now when we were training the prophets. You had to get revelation, and if you didn't get revelation they didn't move.

Prophetic entrepreneurship required a whole lot more and it went beyond the realm of ministry. This was because if we didn't get revelation and keep them studying, they were not going to buy and we would starve.

You know the Lord used our financial situation to make me finish the entire prophetic and apostolic series. If the finances had flowed in before that time we probably would never have finished preaching it.

Ongoing Revelation

Right now I am moving to a new financial level. But it is not going to happen until I am finished teaching and presenting this new course. And everything that I teach here is not coming out of my head. It's not something that I know and have full blown and can say,

"Here it is. Let me tell you everything I know."

I am still learning and still getting revelation. I am journaling every single teaching that I give here. The Prophetic Entrepreneur requires a supernatural anointing from the Holy Spirit in order to function.

We need revelation to put the training schools and the publishing company together. To produce a ministry and now a business resource requires supernatural revelation from the Lord.

God has given training in all the main areas. As He does for the apostle, so He does for the entrepreneur.

Preparation in Different Niches

Finally you need to be prepared in different kinds of niches or groups. I'm going to go through these very quickly.

The Technical Realm

Firstly there is the technical realm which is a very important area. I had exposure in telecommunications, in the laboratory, and also in the waterproofing of buildings. They were all different technical things. And then there was programming of computers.

By Les D. Crause

All of these are different realms. And today computers especially are part of every business. If I did not have the technical know-how, this business and ministry could never have reached the level that it has.

But because God taught me computer programming, I could set up my own web sites and program my own software, instead of having to spend a fortune on other programs out there.

It was a very necessary part of my preparation. All of my technical experiences in all of my jobs brought me to a place where I can stand now as a technical expert.

The Personnel Realm

I had to also get into that Personnel Division. There I learned to write letters because that was part of my job.

Every time a letter needed to be written to an employee, the big boss signed it. But guess who wrote it? It was yours truly, the little clerk down at the bottom. I had to write the nice little letter.

"Dear so-and-so, it has come to our attention that..."

Some of those letters were disciplinary letters that said things like,

"We have been notified that you have been late for work three days in a row. This is not acceptable and it is not part of your job description. And we must warn you that we cannot tolerate this behavior."

You have to learn to say things to people in diplomatic and legal ways. These days it's even more difficult. You have to be politically correct.

Well can you write good letters? I had to go on a letter writing course to learn how to write letters and I got very good at it. Today I write emails all the time, and I don't have to give them to someone else to edit and check out to see if my grammar is correct.

I learned that skill right there as a personnel clerk. I learned how to handle queries from people and how to deal with them.

People would come in and say,

"I was underpaid this month. I hate this company!"

I learned to work with personnel. I learned how to discipline, and how to encourage and motivate people.

Offering Services

I learned how to offer services to people. In the Life Assurance industry it was to offer the service that if you were to die your family would be taken care of. If you should not die, you will be taken care of.

By Les D. Crause

Then of course I had good old ministry training, and that is the ultimate service isn't it? It is called being a servant; in fact God's servant.

You need to offer services to people. Sometimes it is easier to sell a fixed product and say,

"Wouldn't you like one of these? It's so pretty. Would you like it in red, green or blue?"

When you offer someone a service sometimes it's not as easy. But yet it is a very necessary part of the whole business realm.

MLM

There is also good old MLM or selling in a group setting. There you build up your level of commission and attend the conferences where they crank you up and motivate you.

You think, "Isn't it wonderful to be part of this company? Here are all these thousands of people, all making money."

All the big shots who started at the beginning and have built their big pyramids stand up and give you all of their monthly and annual incomes. And you envy them and wish you could reach there one day. It's a different kind of niche altogether.

The Internet

Then the Internet is a niche all on its own isn't it? Here you are setting up websites, producing information products and training courses, and selling by email. That is a whole lot different to selling face to face.

All these different realms come together into one big picture. It is the production of finance for the future as God's entrepreneur. It is putting together a business structure that will tap the resources and the wealth of this world and bring it into the Kingdom of God.

If God has called you to be His entrepreneur you will go through many different kinds of preparation. It is going to vary according to the level of your calling. But don't be surprised if you have been a bit confused.

And when change takes place and you are going in a whole new direction, don't complain and say,

"I can't understand what's going wrong."

It could be that God is taking you through a new phase of your preparation. And when you've been through all the main preparation, then it is time to be trained properly for the office that God has called you to.

Then the training will begin. But that is another story which we will deal with in the next section.

By Les D. Crause

SECTION 03 - THE TRAINING OF AN ENTREPRENEUR

CHAPTER 08

The Phases of Training

Section 03 - The Training of an Entrepreneur

Chapter 08 – The Phases of Training

In the last section we looked at the preparation of an entrepreneur. In that section I shared a lot of my own personal experiences that the Lord took me through in preparing me for this calling to be His entrepreneur.

In this section I would like to now look at the training. I said in the previous section that when preparation is over the training begins. So after preparation comes the training.

The training is very similar to what happens in the ministry realm. The preparation lasts over a long period of time. The training however is intense but a much shorter time than the preparation.

Once you have completed your training then there is qualification. And when this happens you qualify for this office of God's entrepreneur.

How long does this training take? I don't know yet. We have not trained anybody. I have been living this one myself and I have not fully decided when my training began. I do believe however that it has ended because the Lord said it has.

I have a bit of an idea of what happens when it gets to the end. I don't quite know when it started, but I do understand what happened in between.

And so I would like to share with you some of those principles, but not from my own experience now. I have covered enough of that in the preparation.

I'm going to go into the Word, but I will not be using my own experiences to show you the principles that are involved.

I think if you have been through this training you will identify it. And if you have not begun it yet you will know what you are about to go through, because I believe this will be the pattern for the training of God's entrepreneur.

3 Phases of Training

I want to look firstly at the various phases that we go through in the training. There are 3 main phases of training that you will go through as an entrepreneur.

The first phase is a theoretical phase. The second phase is a practical phase. And the third and final phase will be the qualifying phase. Let's look at what happens during these 3 phases very quickly.

By Les D. Crause

The Theoretical Phase

The theoretical phase is the phase during which you are learning principles of doing business God's way. You will do this through a system of education.

You may be doing it through books. You might be doing it through audio or video. Or if you are blessed you could be sitting in a meeting and getting it live, as God gives me the principles and I share them.

Some people will listen to this teaching later in audio format. Some will watch it on video and others will read it in printed form. Whichever form you decide to use, this is your theoretical training phase to become an entrepreneur.

Mentorship

Included with the actual knowledge that is imparted and the principles that you are taught, will be the process of mentorship.

If you are blessed enough to be under our mentorship right now, then you are learning and you are in the training phase right now.

You are learning the theory, being mentored and molded and made into God's entrepreneur.

The Practical Training Phase

Once you have been through your theoretical training there comes the practical training.

Practical training means you now start taking the principles that you have learned and that have been mentored into you. You begin to apply them out there in the field, in the marketplace and in business.

You have to now take what you learned in theory and find out if it really works. You must find out what works and what doesn't work.

You must find out what does or doesn't work in your particular situation. Learn to turn the theory into something practical by gaining experience. Experience always adds to knowledge to create a full understanding and a full training of what is going on.

You have gone through your theoretical phase. Now your practical phase is the phase where you begin to experience all the principles that you have been taught.

The Qualifying Phase

The final phase is the qualifying stage. It is a difficult one, and the one that actually takes the longest period of time. It takes the most difficulty and requires the most from you.

By Les D. Crause

In the qualifying stage, just as in any realm in this world, you have to now be tested. Once you have been through your theory and you have had your hands on practical experience, there comes examination time.

There comes the time when you will be tested to see whether you really understood these principles; to see whether you are ready to actually apply them when things don't always go the way you want them to.

It is the one thing we would love to avoid. And most people who do study courses would love to just go through all the theory. They would love to read the books, watch the videos and write a little examination paper and say,

"That's it; I'm qualified."

There are a lot of qualified people out there who are failing in business, because they have never learned to practically apply the principles. They have never qualified by passing the tests.

If you are going to be God's entrepreneur, let me tell you there are no shortcuts. You have to pass the tests.

Facing the Tests

What kind of tests are you going to face? The first thing I want you to realize is that it is not going to be quite the same as the Ministry Training. You can breathe a sigh of relief now.

The training for an entrepreneur is not a call to death. The entrepreneur does not qualify by failing as you often have to do in ministry, so that is the good news.

The main quality that your training must develop is the one essential quality that will cause you to succeed in business. It is the quality of persistence.

Someone once said that a big shot is just a little shot that kept shooting. The big shot is the hot shot; the guy who thinks he is big.

The one who makes a name for himself started out as a little nobody. But he kept at it and kept pushing at it until one day success broke through.

Persistence is the most important quality of succeeding in this business realm. If you do not keep at it you will fail because the pressures will come against you.

The World System, customers and employees will all come against you. There will be a lot of things that you will face. You must learn not to die and say,

"Well that's it. I can't do it."

No, you must get up and say,

By Les D. Crause

"I learned the principles. I've proved them and they work. I can do this! I'm going to keep pushing until I do it and nothing is going to move me. God is going to give me the grace and I will succeed."

CHAPTER 09

Things You Must Let Go Of

Chapter 09 - Things You Must Let Go Of

Do you want to give up the ministry now and go into business?

Well that statement carries a lot more truth than you realize. Because you see there are some things that you will have to let go of if you want to become God's entrepreneur.

Your Family DNA

The first thing you will have to let go of is your natural family. You will have to give up your family DNA. This is actually the same as the ministry realm.

You might say, "But my dad was a great businessman. My mom was powerful in the marketplace. They taught me such awesome principles and showed me how to succeed."

Give it up if you want to become God's entrepreneur. God is going to teach you to do business His way, not the world's way or mom or dad's way. It is going to be different.

Your Ministry Mandate

You must let go of your natural parents. But there is something else you will have to let go of and that is your spiritual parents.

If you want to be God's entrepreneur and follow the business mandate, here is the bad news. You will have to give up the ministry mandate that you have.

You will not lose your ministry. You won't lose your position in the body of Christ or your gifts of the Spirit. God will still use you, but you are now His entrepreneur.

You are not a business person who is doing ministry on the sideline. Your business has become your ministry. Your business is now your fivefold calling. And as an entrepreneur you are moving to the highest level of calling.

It is going to cost you. If you are not prepared to give up that original desire to go into full time ministry and simply to be a minister for the Lord, then just get a job. Settle down and do your work to the best of your ability using the principles.

You can use many of the principles that we have taught here. But if you are going to become God's entrepreneur you cannot be God's minister at the same time. They are two different things.

By Les D. Crause

God may switch you later from one to the other. That can happen. And many people who are following this business mandate have had a desire for ministry and have perhaps even been through our ministry training.

Perhaps you have even been placed in a ministry office. If you want to become God's entrepreneur you will have to let that go. If you have spiritual parents you will also have to leave them behind.

Natural and Spiritual Children

Next you will have to let go of every person that is under you and that you have parented.

You will have to let go of all your natural children, your responsibilities and obligations to your own family and leave them behind. And if you have spiritual children you will also have to let them go.

There must be no more being a PI; no more chiseling and trying to mold and change them in any way.

They were your spiritual children, but there are no spiritual children under the business mandate. There are also no spiritual parents under the business mandate. I am sure that shocked you.

You have to let it go. I will show you from the Scriptures the pattern that is there.

You will have to let go of those that are above you as parents and spiritual parents. And you are going to have to let go of those that are below you as natural and spiritual children.

Dealing With the Flesh

And then you will have to deal with fleshly desires. This is because the business realm is not the realm of the spirit.

When you are in the realm of the spirit and in the ministry, you are walking with the Lord day by day. You are walking in His Spirit, ministering and preaching, and when you do that the flesh automatically falls away.

You are not dealing with those temptations anymore. But now suddenly you are in a worldly environment.

You are rubbing shoulders with unbelievers in a worldly situation, and most of your work all day is not primarily a spiritual thing.

You are doing it God's way and are using spiritual power, and you will still use the anointing of God to accomplish this.

Even though you are doing these things, there is now a greater temptation that will come upon you. The desires of the flesh will suddenly burst forth in a way that you never faced before when you were in ministry.

By Les D. Crause

Relationships Issues

You will find a new challenge coming in the realm of relationships. You know there are affairs that take place in churches, but it doesn't happen very often. And when it does the pastor gets kicked out.

But relationships and affairs take place all the time in the business realm. This is because you are mixing with members of the opposite sex and there are pressures that come upon the flesh.

There are temptations that you will face in the business realm that you never faced in the spiritual realm. And the pressure will be upon you to stand firm as a child of God and refuse to give in to sin, because the temptation will be there.

If you are a wealthy businessman rising up with a lot of money, there are many beautiful women out there who would like to get their hands on that money. They would like to be in the position of being the wife of the boss.

Yes it happens in churches too. But unless someone is a Jezebel, it is not so easy for them to lure the pastor away in the church.

But it is so easy in the business realm, where every day you are mixing with women who come to work beautifully dressed. And because you are the boss they smile sweetly and do exactly what you say.

They make a fuss of you and make you feel good about yourself. Then you go home to a wife who doesn't do that.

The temptation is very strong in the business realm. And if you want to move into business, watch out for it because it is going to happen.

You are going to face temptations in the realm of the flesh, and you will fall unless you take a firm stand with the Lord's help. Don't think it's going to be a simple matter of saying,

"Well I can see she's a bit of a slut. She's just trying to get me to bed."

No, that isn't the woman that you fall for. It is the one who really is your right hand.

Why do you think most managing directors and bosses end up having affairs with their secretaries? It is because they spend time with their secretaries and they share their hearts with them.

The secretary listens and understands and ministers to their need. Then they go home and the wife doesn't do that.

There is a very strong pull, not to lust, but you find yourself drawn to a woman who really cares for you and understands you in a way that your wife doesn't.

By Les D. Crause

It can happen with women too. It doesn't only happen to men, but men have a stronger tug to the sexual side. Women are not exempt from this though.

A woman in the marketplace faces the exact same pressures when she has a husband who perhaps feels threatened by her position. As a result he doesn't affirm her and lift her up, and make her feel good about herself when she comes home.

And so in the work place she responds to other men who make a fuss of her and make her feel good about herself as a woman.

It is a pressure and you will face this one. It is not a case of you maybe facing it. You **will** face this one as you move into the business realm and as you get involved with people in the marketplace.

Openness in Your Marriage

Your marriage will be challenged. And there is a danger of you keeping your wife apart from your business.

This seems very good practice because you don't want to involve her in the business. You don't want her to face the pressures that you face in the business realm, so you shield her from it by keeping her out there.

But by keeping her out there she is not able to understand what you are going through. She isn't able to minister to your needs when you come home stressed at night.

So you wait until the next day when the secretary is there because she really understands you. She is in the workplace and she knows what you are doing. She can see it.

Don't **ever** isolate your spouse from your business involvement. Don't ever try and do it on your own and put your spouse one side. It will destroy your marriage.

You may become very wealthy and make a lot of money. But you will lose the most important possession that you have in your life - your wife or your husband that the Lord has given to you.

Temporal Values

Next there is the pull of temporal values. You have to entertain in business. You must take customers out to lunch and create a social environment in order to make them happy and to make business deals.

You are going to eat too much and you will put on weight. Have you ever seen wealthy businessmen that are skinny or wealthy businesswomen that look like models? Not if they have fully commit themselves to the whole social thing.

By Les D. Crause

How can you go on a diet and control what you eat when you have to do this as part of your work situation?

There is going to be a pressure on you. You will not have time to exercise and to keep your body healthy and in trim.

You will end up putting on weight. You'll end up with cholesterol, ruining your health and probably dying early in spite of your wealth.

The desire for things can so consume you and drive you that you have to make more and more money. And even then that is not enough.

You say, "We have all this money in the bank but it's not enough. We need more. I can't live with this amount. I have to be wealthier. I have to drive a better car and live in a better house."

There comes the pull of temporal values which drives you, and you lose the fact that you are not just a business owner. You are God's entrepreneur, and you are not raising finance to cater to your own fleshly desires.

The Lord will give you everything you desire. But you are there as an instrument for the Kingdom of God. Don't ever forget it.

No Aggression

There is a temptation to be over-defensive and aggressive. This is especially true when you are dealing with the opposition, with competitive companies and products.

You get all bitter and twisted. You lash out, attack and try to destroy.

That is not the spirit of Christ. Yes competition is good. Praise the Lord for competition, otherwise businesses would charge what they want and give poor service.

If you want to compete with somebody else then give better service. Give better prices and better products. Give according to the principles that we have taught in many teachings.

You have to deal with competitiveness on the job, with different employees competing with one another and vying for higher positions.

These are all things that happen. And even if you yourself are working say as the manager of a branch of a company that has other branches around the country, there is the competition to rise up into higher management.

You become aggressive and you want to attack and tear down the person who stands in your way.

By Les D. Crause

These are the temptations you will face as an entrepreneur in the marketplace.

Pressures in the Workplace

Finally you will have to learn to work under pressure. If you cannot work under pressure you cannot survive in the marketplace. You will not survive in the realm of business, because out there it is dog eat dog.

Demands on Your Time

There will be pressure from people making demands on your time. If you are the business owner you are not working from 9 to 5. You could be working from 6 to 11 or longer.

You have responsibilities, but people will gladly make demands on your time and think nothing of it. They don't care. They want their needs met first.

People will drain you and make demands on your time. You will have to learn to schedule your time and to get done what needs to be done in the time that is available to you.

You will have to exercise control and persistence to push through. Especially during this time of training, suddenly everyone will be calling on your time. Suddenly there will be no time to do anything and you will say,

"I can't understand what is happening. We were doing great. Things were going well and suddenly now all hell is let loose. What is going on?"

Welcome to the training of an entrepreneur. That is what is happening.

Demands on Your Resources

There will be demands on your resources. Suddenly everybody in the company will need you to make a decision for them.

You will be handling hundreds of emails and interviews every day. People will be calling you on the phone every day.

You will barely have time to have lunch. There will be demands upon your resources, your skill and your wisdom.

It will drain the life out of you. You will come home exhausted in the evening and will be so tired you won't even be able to sleep. You will get up the next day still feeling exhausted and having to face another day like that.

If you have been going through that it might just be that you have officially begun entrepreneurial training.

By Les D. Crause

Demands on Your Finances

There will be demands on your finances. New bills will suddenly come up, and you will need new equipment because some of it will be breaking down.

You will have people demanding pay increases. There will be all sorts of demands on your finances. Suddenly the money will be going out faster than what it is coming in.

What is going on? You are in entrepreneurial training.

Rearranging Schedules

Then you have your wonderful schedule that you had organized so nicely. You say that you will arrive at work at this time, check your emails, get this done and then do that.

You say, "This is the morning. We have this to do and then we have a few meetings organized. Then we have a lunch time."

It will be all nicely organized and suddenly your whole schedule will get messed up.

Suddenly people will want to see you at awkward times, and you will have to cancel appointments and change your schedule. It seems that you just don't know what you are doing anymore.

The whole of the last week has gone and you feel like you have accomplished nothing. You have been running here, running there and putting out fires.

Has that been happening to you? Welcome to entrepreneurial training.

Time to Qualify

These are the things that will qualify you. This is testing time. The good news is that it is not going to last forever, because when you qualify it will come together and you will understand what has been happening.

Suddenly you will see the whole picture and you will say,

"I just thought the enemy was getting in and that Satan was having a hay day with me in this business. I thought maybe I sinned somewhere or did something wrong. What is going on Lord?"

The Lord says, "You wanted to be my entrepreneur didn't you?"

"Yes."

"Well it is called training."

It is examination time. We are putting you through this crash course so that you can qualify, rise up and become that wonderful leader in the realm of business that you've desired to be.

By Les D. Crause

CHAPTER 10

Four Entrepreneurs from Scripture

Chapter 10 - Four Entrepreneurs from Scripture

I would like to look very quickly at some Scriptural examples. I am not going to go into a lot of detail because I have other teachings that deal with these in detail.

On the ministry side there were four different apostolic types. In the same way on the business side there are four different entrepreneurial types.

We chose four Bible characters as being symbols of the apostolic calling and the various different apostolic types. Now in the same way there are four Bible characters which are symbols of the four entrepreneurial types.

They are not ordinary entrepreneurs, but God's entrepreneurs. We will look at these in detail as we continue. For now I will just give you their names.

The first one is Abraham. The second one is Jacob. The third one is Joseph. And the fourth one is Solomon.

You might say to me,

"Hang on, wasn't Solomon one of the apostolic types?"

How very observant of you. Yes Solomon was one of the Apostolic Ministry types.

Solomon actually bridges the Apostolic Ministry and the entrepreneurial leadership. And together if you count it you don't have eight apostolic types because Solomon has both.

There are actually seven. Isn't that amazing? Seven is God's number of perfection.

Sevenfold Apostolic Leadership

Here is something that you have likely never heard before which I deal with in more detail in Section 06. We have looked at the fivefold calling as well as the fourfold apostolic types. Now I want to show you a brand new set: the sevenfold apostolic leadership of the body of Christ.

This includes three apostles and three entrepreneurs. One of them is both an apostle and an entrepreneur and that is Solomon.

We will be looking at Solomon in a whole lot more detail. But for now I want to take these four entrepreneurial types and just look at a few highlights and experiences from their lives that line up with some of the principles that we covered now on training.

Abraham

Let's look at Abraham. Where did Abraham learn his theory?

Letting Go of All Family

Well God told him to give up whatever he learned from his dad. He said to Abraham,

"Leave behind your father, your father's house and your family."

Abraham grew up there in Ur of the Chaldees; a heathen nation. Now I'm sure Abraham had some very good business principles, because later on you can see he understood a bit about business.

The Bible doesn't tell us, but let me tell you he had to give up his father, his family, and everything that he received from being born into that family.

Then he had to let go of the person who was under him; his spiritual son if you wish. It was his nephew Lot that he dragged along with him. He had to let him go as well.

He thought, "Well I'll let go of my father, but I'll hang onto Lot because he can be of use to me. He knows how I think and we can do things together."

He also faced pressures in his marriage. He didn't cover his wife or involve her in what he was doing. And when he faced the pressure he said to her,

"We're going somewhere where there could be trouble. Please lie for me and say that you are not my wife but rather my sister."

He got into trouble. He faced some tests and he passed most of them.

Pressure and Conflict

There was conflict with Lot and Abraham said,

"We are going to have to separate. We will have to split the land between us."

He was the senior one. He could have taken the best land and said,

"Okay Lot, you can have that little piece of dirty grassland that's not much use to anybody. Be thankful that I gave you something, but I'm the uncle here. I'm the senior and I have got it. God gave me this land."

No, he stood back and he said,

"Okay Lot, you choose first."

Of course Lot, being the young upstart, thought he knew it all. He jumped in and took the best land, with all the wealth and the riches and the opportunities for business. He left Abraham with this miserable farmland.

You see Abraham passed a test there. He didn't allow temporal values to control him, because he had a call and a mandate from God, and God had promised him,

"I'm going to give you a promised land."

By Les D. Crause

He didn't have to worry or fear. He knew that his business was dedicated to the Lord, and he didn't care what the opposition took. He didn't care what his family, his spiritual children or anyone else took. God was his source.

He faced a lot of pressure. Both he and Lot had herdsmen for their flocks. Their herdsmen were always bickering and fighting and he was always caught in the middle of it.

I think Abraham was a bit of a pacifist. He was very much an analytical. I really don't think he liked to confront and face pressure, but he certainly had pressure.

But you know when he was finished God said to him,

"Okay, this is the land that I've given you. This is how I am going to bless you and what I'm going to give you. You have qualified Abraham, now step into the calling that I have given to you."

Jacob

Then there was Jacob. Where did he learn from?

It is difficult to know where Jacob learned from in his youth. But it could not have been the Lord at first, because he was a cheat and a liar who cheated his brother out of his inheritance and his blessing.

Working for His Uncle

Jacob had great ideas and great zeal. He was going to conquer the world. He was going to become wealthy and have all these things, but he didn't know how to go about it. So God sent him down to Uncle Laban.

He had to leave his family behind. He had to leave his dad and mom behind and never ever see her again so it really cost him.

But there with Uncle Laban he learned some things. A lot of the time he learned how *not* to do things. I'm sure that he learned a bit as he watched and worked for him.

He had quite a few years to do that in, and then he realized,

"This knowledge is not enough. I need to learn from a higher source."

Getting Revelation from God

Jacob learned to hear from God and get revelation from Him. He learned some principles that no business person had ever taught before; things that his Uncle Laban didn't even understand.

He took those principles and he put them into practice, using the most absurd method you could ever think of.

He said, "I'll take all the spotted and speckled sheep."

By Les D. Crause

Well how often does a spotted or speckled sheep get born? It only happens once in a while.

He said, "I'll just take that Uncle Laban. That's all you need to pay me."

What Uncle Laban didn't know was that Jacob had a business plan. It was a very weird business plan and we are not going to go into that in detail.

But he had this plan and his flock began to multiply and multiply. And before you knew it he had more cattle and sheep than what his uncle did.

He took those principles that God had taught him and applied them practically. He found out that they worked and he built his business.

Yes he went through the qualification time. He had to leave his father and mother. And he had to face the anger of his brother and humble himself to go back and apologize to his brother.

Inspired by Women

Jacob worked really hard, not smart, because of women. The whole temporal thing was there. What a man will do for a beautiful woman. He saw Rachel and said,

"Oh wow, I must have her."

Uncle Laban was a very shrewd businessman and he said to Jacob,

"Sure, work for me for seven years and you can have her."

After seven years he was given her sister instead and he had to work another seven years. The whole appeal of the opposite sex can actually be a very good thing and it can be used well.

God can use it to give you an incentive to push on and to qualify, but there is going to be pressure along the way. Year after year Jacob worked really hard. Laban changed his wages again and again, until one day he woke up and said,

"It's time for me to do it God's way."

When he made that decision God said,

"Okay you're qualified. Let's do it."

Jacob then went off, rose up and became a wealthy business owner.

Joseph

Let's move on to Joseph now. Where did Joseph learn what he knew?

Well all that he learned was watching his brothers look after the flock. And he was probably just the little skivvy that did all the dirty work because his brothers were older than him.

But he learned humbly. He was the little shepherd boy. Of course dad made a big fuss of him and gave him the fancy coat so he thought he was a bit of a hotshot.

I can see Joseph going to his brothers and saying,

"Why don't you try it that way?"

And I can imagine them saying,

"Come on you stupid little idiot, what do you know about looking after sheep?"

But he must have learned something during that time.

Training Time

And then God gave him an opportunity, by special invitation, to become a slave with Potiphar. Here he suddenly had the opportunity to work in a real business.

He had the chance to work his way up and to be put in charge of the business. He saw how a man who accumulated wealth worked, and how things should and shouldn't be done.

I think during that time in Potiphar's house, Joseph had an immense theoretical and practical training. He especially had a theoretical training as he watched how Potiphar did things.

Afterwards when he was thrown into prison, that was when Joseph got his true training.

When you are sitting in prison for years you have nothing much else to do except talk to God, because He is probably the only one there who listens to you.

He already had the ability to receive revelation. And during that period in obscurity, Joseph learned all the principles that he later put into practice when he rose up under Pharaoh and became the ruler of Egypt.

He put those principles into practice from the moment he interpreted Pharaoh's dream, and Pharaoh said,

"That's a brilliant idea, Joseph. You're in charge."

Putting it into Practice

Joseph probably had a chance to prove what he had learned with Potiphar and maybe even what he learned with his father's flocks. But he had a chance to put into practice especially what God had taught him.

He learned how to accumulate all the resources during the time of plenty. And then when the famine came he went into awesome business practice and ended up owning most of Egypt.

That is a good businessman for you. He learned to apply the principles practically.

How did Joseph qualify? I want to tell you that it cost him big time. He was daddy's blue-eyed boy. Whatever he wanted, daddy gave him. I think if he told on his brothers daddy believed him over them.

Facing Temptations

Joseph had it made - so God took away dad by sending him off to be sold as a slave. And yes he faced the desires of the flesh. He faced the temptations.

Here he was in Potiphar's employment, and the only thing that he didn't have access to was Potiphar's most prized possession - his wife. And here the wife came and offered herself to him on a platter.

She said, "Here, you can have me too."

What a temptation. You are in charge of everything and you can have the boss's wife as well. It was the ultimate temptation. For all you know she was the one who ruled the business anyway.

Very often that is the case. The man may hold the position, but the wife really is the one who owns the business. Her dad perhaps gave it to her, then she married him and he took it over and ran it. You often have that situation.

It could have been a golden opportunity for him. Logically it could have made sense. But he did not give in to sin, because he was God's entrepreneur.

Because of that he faced the ultimate pressure. He was thrown into prison and had to sit there and be misunderstood.

Yes they soon recognized his potential and put him in charge of all the other prisoners. What a lot of use that was though. He helped everybody else, they served their time, then they went out and never even mentioned him.

He worked hard interpreting the dreams for them. Then they went out and didn't even mention his name to Pharaoh.

Pressure, stress, a call on your time - Joseph faced all of these things. But he came to that place of hanging in there and not giving up.

He was not going to give up on the Lord or on his vision. He still had that dream, and the visions that he had as a child still burned in him. He kept pushing until it was God's time and the Lord said,

By Les D. Crause

"Okay you've qualified. It's time for promotion, Joseph. You step out of prison and into the highest position in the land."

Solomon

Finally we look at Solomon. Where did Solomon learn the theory? It is difficult to tell, because Solomon kind of appeared on the scene suddenly and unexpectedly.

He was obviously a reader and very intellectual. He was probably an analytical type, because later on you see him spending so much time accumulating knowledge.

It is difficult to tell how much knowledge he had when he became king. But I'm sure by then he had studied a bit of something. He certainly must have looked at what his father was doing and saw what his brothers were doing.

Receiving Wisdom

Solomon had lived a few years, but we don't really know what kind of theoretical study he did. We do know however, that when he came to the throne he said,

"Lord I need wisdom."

God said, "Here you go."

Solomon received an instant degree overnight. Wow, how do you go from being an ordinary Joe to the wisest man who ever lived? It takes God to do that.

How do you go from being an ordinary employee to being a highly successful business entrepreneur? It takes God. If God has called you to be His entrepreneur, He will give you the wisdom that you need.

His Time with David

Solomon had a limited time with his father, but basically David left him behind. He had to leave dad behind.

Dad was so busy fighting wars that he didn't have time to sit down with his son and explain to him what it was like to be a king.

In fact he was so old he forgot that he had promised that Solomon would be king. His wife had to come and remind him, because his older brother Adonijah was about to get in there and take the throne.

Suddenly David woke up and said,

"Oh yes, I forgot. Solomon is meant to be king."

He only had a short time to suddenly mentor Solomon and prepare him. And when Solomon stepped onto the throne he didn't have much practical experience yet.

Dealing with Different People

Look what he had to deal with as he stepped onto the throne. David had given him directions and had said,

"Solomon, kill all the bad guys that I never had the courage to kill."

"Thanks dad that's great. So how do I do that?"

"Just kill them. You're going to be the king. You must deal with them Solomon."

Do you know who the guys were that he was meant to kill? They were the top leaders in the land; the strong guys who had years and years of experience.

There was the priest who was in charge of everything, and his dad's uncle who ran the whole army. They were all the top guys.

Then there was his older brother, the good looking guy who had all the people behind him. These were the people he had to kill. There was nobody big.

He also had to deal with ordinary people. Well he grew up as the king's son. I'm sure he didn't have much time to play with other kids. But suddenly here he was on the throne and there were all these ordinary peasants coming to him for help and advice.

Whatever he had learned in theory, and especially whatever God had given him in wisdom, now had a chance to be tested practically.

Business Opportunity

And then it came to real business. One of the top business owners and businessmen of that time was the king of Tyre and Sidon, king Hiram. He was the leader of the whole enterprise that rocked the world.

He came to Solomon to congratulate him on becoming king and said,

"I liked your dad. We had a good relationship. I just wanted to come and give you my blessing and tell you I'm here for you."

Solomon jumped at the idea immediately. He was no fool. He knew here was someone who had experience; someone who could mentor him and show him a bit about the business.

It took a while for Hiram to mentor him. And as always happens, the disciple rises above his master. Solomon became a far greater business person even than Hiram.

How did he qualify? Well dad gave him very little to work with in training. But he obeyed and got rid of those people.

Solomon had an interfering mother who tried to push him into doing something he shouldn't do, like giving Abishag to his older brother to be a wife. He could see that it was a ploy; an attempt to take away his authority on the throne.

By Les D. Crause

Well how do you stand against this and not upset mom? You see there was a temptation. There was family influence that he had to give up and let go of.

But he failed on the other temptation - the desires of the flesh. Fortunately he was king and he could get as many women as he liked. Nobody said to him,

"You can't have more than one wife. Hey, 10 wives is enough."

He was king. He could have 1000 if that's what he wanted. And ultimately that was Solomon's downfall in the end. But in the beginning he gave God the glory.

Pressures and Tests

Solomon faced pressure and had opposition from all the strong leaders. He had the needs of all the people, and he even had international calls on his wisdom. People came from all over the world to ask him for wisdom.

He had the Queen of Sheba coming to test him. We don't really know what happened, but I know the entertainers like to say that Solomon had something going with the Queen of Sheba and they had a relationship.

Perhaps she was beautiful. Perhaps he did even have a relationship with her. Strong pressure came upon Solomon before he could rise up and be God's entrepreneur.

The Three Temptations

So what is the end result of training? There are three things:

1. Wealth
2. Fame
3. Authority

Do you recognize those three things? They are the temptations that Jesus faced in the Wilderness. They are also the temptations that every leader faces.

I taught in the apostolic teaching that these are the three temptations that the apostle will face and the three tests that he must pass.

And in the end in the realm of ministry you have to give up all desire for wealth. You have to give up all desire for fame. You are to be God's servant, and He will lift you up in His time.

For the entrepreneur these are your goals. This is what you are aiming for. That is why you have to be tested. It is why you have to pass those tests and you have to qualify before God can trust you with untold wealth.

You must do this before He can lift you up on high and put you on a pinnacle, where everybody can see you and you become famous.

By Les D. Crause

You must do this before He can trust you to have authority over other people, to run their lives and tell them what to do. But this is the result of your training.

If you have qualified and have been through your training, expect to get wealthy. If you've been through your training and qualified, expect to become better known and more famous.

If you have qualified in your training, expect to get greater authority and more people under you, because these are the natural consequences and results of qualifying to be God's entrepreneur.

Wrapping it Up

In conclusion then, the training of an entrepreneur always follows three stages.

Firstly there is the theoretical stage. Learn all that you can from books, audio and video; from mentors and from every source that you can.

The second stage is the practical stage. Try the principles out and make them your own. Individuate in this. Make them more than principles that somebody else taught you.

They must now become your own principles. You add your own experience to them and they become your own practical knowledge.

And then finally face the tests. Push through to victory until you qualify.

Symbols of Qualification

On completion of training to qualify you will receive three things. The first one is a crown. Yes, just like the apostle there is a crown. What is a crown? It is the ability to rule.

The second one is a staff, just like Moses' staff. This is the ability to become famous by doing amazing things; to originate new ideas and go where no man or entrepreneur has gone before.

And finally you will receive a golden sword, which symbolizes the ability to create wealth.

You will receive these three things but I believe there may be others. In the past we learned by experience that as we began to train people we would see other objects that God gives. But these are the first three that I have seen that are given to the entrepreneur who qualifies.

So there is a goal for you to aim for. Somebody may pray with you one day. They may give you these three things and say,

"I see the Lord putting these three things on you."

By Les D. Crause

If this happens, it could be an indication that you just qualified and were placed into this office of entrepreneur.

Before you get there however, you must have been through the preparation and you have to go through your time of training.

Section 04 – The Business Anointing

Chapter 11

What the Business Anointing is

Section 04 – The Business Anointing

Chapter 11 – What the Business Anointing is

Deuteronomy 8:17 and 18 says,

*And [if] you say in your heart, My strength and my natural ability have produced this wealth.
Then you should remember that the LORD [Yahweh] your God is the one who gives you the anointing and power and anointing to produce prosperity and wealth, so that he may confirm his covenant which he swore to your fathers, which still stands today.*

There are two areas of confusion which every one of us as believers face when we set out on the road of life. The first question we have to ask is,

"What ministry has God called me to?"

Most people are confused about it. They are unsure and really don't know what God has called them to. They don't know what their ministry should be, and it takes them a while to figure it out.

The second question is,

"What job career should I follow?"

Every one of us knows what that one is about, especially round about the time we leave school. People start saying,

"So what are you going to do?"

Adults often say to kids,

"What are you going to be when you grow up?"

You have all these big ideas, but when it finally faces you suddenly you're in the throws and you say,

"What am I going to do? What do I really want to do? Where do I get direction from and what is the wise thing to do right now?"

You see in the past, as believers we have always tried to find the answers to these questions in two different places.

If you want to find out what your ministry is you go to church. You consult with the spiritual leaders to try and find out what your ministry is, and to be trained for the calling that God has put on your life. We are used to doing that as Christians.

But what do you do when it comes to your job career and the secular part of your life; the part that you do outside of church?

By Les D. Crause

You go to the world and you ask the world's advice on what you should do. And you ask the world to train and equip you for what will probably take a larger part of your life than the little bit of time you will spend in church.

There's an imbalance. Something is wrong. God is about to change that in the end times church in a very wonderful and significant way. This is what I want to share with you about in this section.

Conflict of Interests

Usually when you face these two things in your life a conflict takes place. The one seems so spiritual but the other seems so carnal.

It is almost as though we kind of play the one against the other. If you really feel the call to ministry you think,

"How can I follow a career? God has called me. I should only be thinking about ministry. How can I think about a job?

How can I study and qualify in something secular and natural, spending all my time and effort doing worldly things, when I should be getting ready?

The Lord is coming soon. We need to reach the world. We're going to turn the world upside down."

If you are a young person and you have felt the call of God for the first time, you want to go and conquer the world. Who has time to go to College and study?

Who has time to go and settle down in a normal job? You have to get into the ministry tomorrow.

Then suddenly you find out that you have to eat and you have to live. You never got into a job and you are not qualified in anything, and now suddenly there is a financial dilemma. You say,

"How can I afford to go into ministry without money?"

People say, "Don't worry brother, the Lord will provide. Just live by faith."

That is easier said than done. But you know why? We have gone and separated our ministry call from our secular call.

We've looked to the Lord for the one and to the world for the other. We didn't realize that God actually wants to be in charge of both.

And then there is that difficult situation where you just don't have a call.

You say, "It's not fair. Everybody else has a call to the ministry but I don't. I'm just a second rate Christian. I am a failure who is useless to the Lord. All I can do is get an ordinary job while everyone else is going into the ministry."

All of these conflict situations occur quite simply because we are not following these two roads God's way.

A Lot of Confusion

So where do you draw the line between a career in business and a career in ministry? That is the way we see it don't we?

We see that our career is either going to be in the secular world in business. Or our career is going to be full time ministry for the Lord, and that becomes your job.

Should we really be choosing between these two? Is that what the Lord really intends? It has caused so much confusion and so much heartache and difficulty.

Then there are those poor people who give it all up to go into the ministry and fall on their faces. Suddenly they find out they never qualified in anything in the secular. Their whole life is a failure and they are no use to God or man.

The Business Anointing

I would like to share about the anointing of God. And specifically in this section I would like to share with you about the business anointing.

You have never likely heard that term before, because no preacher has ever stood up and preached about the business anointing. And if they did they gave it in a faulty way.

So let's look at the anointing of God and see if we can understand how the anointing is meant to operate in our lives. Let's see how it should work in both ministry and in business, because that is what God intends.

What the Anointing is

What is the anointing of God and how does it work?

Well if you have studied the ministry side you will be able to give me all the answers. You might say that it is very easy to understand what ministry is. Is it really? What is the anointing of God?

Something Supernatural

Firstly the anointing of God is supernatural. It is not natural.

That immediately puts the secular side out doesn't it, because it requires supernatural power to do ministry. But anybody with natural ability can go out and get a good job, make money and do business.

You say, "All it takes is natural skill, natural intelligence and natural personality doesn't it?"

By Les D. Crause

Does it really? The anointing is a gift of God. It's not something that you earn. It is not something like a course that you can pay for, go and qualify and get a certificate. It is a gift of God.

The anointing also gives you abilities that you did not have before you received the anointing.

The anointing is not taking your natural abilities and developing them. The anointing is God-given supernatural power that gives you abilities and allows you to do things that you couldn't do before in the natural.

The anointing also enhances the capabilities of our human spirit, because there is if you like 'natural' power in the spirit. We have called it the latent power of the spirit.

This is in us because God put His very nature into us. And as the anointing comes upon us, God takes that which is in our spirits, which He put there in the first place, and He enhances and increases it.

This is how the anointing works and it comes from only one source. It comes from God Himself in the form of the Holy Spirit. The Holy Spirit is the one who anoints us.

Different Kinds of Anointing

There are different kinds of anointing. We have looked at that plenty of times under the ministry side. We have realized that there are different anointings for different ministries and we have done a lot of teaching on that.

We have looked at this Scripture from 1 Corinthians 12:4 to 7 which says,

Now there are various different gifts, but the same Spirit. There are various different ways of serving, but the same Lord.
And there are various different effects created, but it is the same God that energizes all [of them] in all [cases]. But the manifestation of the Spirit is given so that everyone can benefit.

Not all gifts are the same. There are different kinds of gifts. You don't say,

"I have the gift of the Holy Spirit."

Yes the Holy Spirit was God's gift to you. But resident in the Holy Spirit are various different kinds of manifestations of different gifts, and they manifest in different ways at different times.

Different functions require different gifts don't they? We've seen on the ministry side that certain gifts operate more under different ministry functions.

You don't use all the gifts for everything. Well maybe you could. But generally you find that according to the kind of function you get involved in in the body of Christ, you tend to operate in different gifts at different times.

By Les D. Crause

The gifts also bring different results depending on where they are used. Depending on the circumstance or the situation you are operating and functioning in, those gifts can produce a different kind of result.

If that gift is operating in a ministry of evangelism, the result you want is to see souls getting saved. If it is operating in a ministry of healing you want to see bodies being healed.

Anointing not Only for Ministry

Whatever kind of function you are in, the anointing enables you to bring about results that match the particular function that you are carrying out.

I am using the term function now instead of ministry, because ministry speaks of servanthood. It speaks of working for a boss or having a job to do.

Well is that only a job to do for the Lord? Are you only ministering when the job that you're doing is with God as your boss directly? What about when you are working for a human boss? You are still serving and doing a job.

Is it possible that the anointing of God can help you in every function in life, not just those functions that involve spiritual ministry in the church and in the body of Christ?

What the Business Anointing is

The anointing of God is so wide and so varied. But we've limited it, restricted it and narrowed it down to this little area that we call the ministry.

You say, "I have been believing God for the anointing."

I know that weak, frail little me, who can hardly open my mouth to speak, when the anointing comes on me I get to stand up behind the pulpit to preach and the power of God begins to move.

You know that the anointing gives you the wisdom when you are counseling and sharing with someone about the Lord, and when you're doing something for the extension of the Kingdom of God.

We know the anointing and how it works in those situations. But when we get into the secular side, into business and our daily work functions, we leave the anointing at home.

The exception is if in the middle of our work, we somehow bump into someone and begin to share the gospel. As we begin to share the Word we think,

"Would you believe it? The anointing came with me to work. I'm still anointed."

Then we finish ministering to somebody spiritually. We get back to talking about the job and the anointing is gone again, right?

By Les D. Crause

It shouldn't be that way because there is also a business anointing. The business anointing operates in a very similar way. It does exactly the same thing.

Firstly it energizes you to carry out business activities rather than ministry activities. It is the same supernatural power of God.

It is the same ability that you don't have naturally and that God gives you supernaturally. And now it enables you to do something efficiently in the secular world.

This is not something you are born with. It comes from the Holy Spirit because it is an anointing. And the anointing is always 100 percent supernatural. It comes from God.

Chapter 12

An Anointing for Business Success

Chapter 12 – An Anointing for Business Success

Who the Anointing is For

Who is this anointing available to? Who has the business calling? Well let's answer this question. Who is the ministry anointing available to? Who has the calling to ministry?

It is available to every single one of us. The Scripture says that the manifestation of God is given to every person to benefit from. This anointing is available to every single believer.

You say, "That's fine; you're called to business and I'm called to ministry. So perhaps you can have the business anointing and I can have the ministry anointing.

We'll each go on our own road and keep these two separate because they are different kinds of anointing."

Yes they are different kinds of anointing. But you see you still have the old idea that you are either going to follow a career in ministry, or you are going to follow a career in business.

But most Christians are not in full time ministry. Most Christians are not in the fivefold leadership offices in the church. They are ordinary believers but they have a ministry.

They have a function to carry out in the body of Christ. And they need the anointing of God in order to do that.

Every Christian has a job to do. They have a responsibility to put bread on the table and to earn an income for their family. The Scripture says,

If any man will not work, neither let him eat.

Every believer has available to them the anointing of God to enable them to supernaturally do their work under God's power. That gives us a whole new dimension doesn't it?

The Anointing for Success

What is the result of the business anointing? It is wealth and prosperity. Don't confuse those two although they are the same thing. Wealth and prosperity do not necessarily mean money.

The verse we looked at in the beginning said,

It is God who gives you the power and anointing to produce wealth.

I looked up that word wealth in the Hebrew in Strongs, and these are the kinds of meanings that that word has:

1. Strength
2. Ability
3. Efficiency
4. Wealth
5. Force
6. Army

It is much wider than just making money. It is the power to be successful in whatever you do. It's the power to rise up; to be more efficient and to have greater ability and strength.

Yes it is to create money but not just money. It is the ability to accumulate possessions; to accumulate a position and to get fame and fortune. This is the power of prosperity that God has promised us by His Spirit under this business anointing.

So the anointing is not just to make money. The anointing is to make us more efficient. And when we become more efficient and we work better then what happens?

If you are working for a boss you are going to get a pay increase. If you're working in your own business you are going to get more sales.

You are going to prosper, increase and expand. You are going to become better and more efficient, because you are operating under the anointing power of God.

When you leave for work in the morning you don't think,

"I wish I was in ministry so that I could spend the whole day in the anointing."

You get out there and you say,

"I'm going to work in the anointing today. Wait until those customers see me. They're going to be hit by the power of God.

They will be pulling out their wallets and throwing their money at me. Everyone will be amazed that I'm doing the job better than they are."

Isn't that the way it should be?

Blessing on My Job

I remember the last secular job that I had. I had been in ministry for a long time, and now the Lord had told me to pack up the ministry and go back into secular work.

I thought, "Oh Lord I can't wait to get back into ministry again."

The Lord said to me,

"When you join this company, this business is going to boom and prosper just because you are there. I am going to bring the blessing and anointing on you."

You know I couldn't believe it. I struggled for the first month, taking over from another guy who knew what he was doing. I had barely a month to learn his job and I knew virtually nothing when I took over.

That was bad enough, but that month was the biggest production the company had ever had. They had more sales than they ever had and there were more customers to see to than ever before. It nearly killed me.

When I complained to the Lord He said,

"I told you I was going to bless this business."

My boss said to me the one day,

"We've never had this many sales this time of the year. I can't understand what's happening."

I knew what was happening. The blessing of God was on me. I didn't know it then, but I was operating in the business anointing, but I couldn't wait to go back into ministry. It was stupid.

Eventually I was so blessed that I had to do after hours work with extra customers and a second income, to try and cope with all the work that was coming my way. It was the business anointing that was operating on me.

Using the Gifts in Business

You see it takes the power of God. This anointing is going to involve using the gifts of the Spirit. It will give you supernatural power, because there are power gifts amongst the gifts of the Spirit.

It is going to allow you supernatural revelation. You will see things in the work situation, understand things and know what to do, all by the supernatural revelation that will come via the gift of revelation.

Even your vocal powers are going to be improved. There are vocal gifts that allow you to speak, and God will take control of your lips.

When you start giving a sales pitch, you will feel like you are ministering the gospel to someone, because suddenly the sales will start to take place. You will think,

"The last time that happened was when I led somebody to the Lord."

It is the business anointing.

You might say, "But God never called me to business. I'm a prophet."

You are a Christian aren't you? We will get to the business leadership calling shortly. But I'm talking about an anointing from God that is available to every single one of us as His children.

This will enable us to prosper in everything that we touch. It will help us to succeed in the workplace, in the natural secular world using the power of God.

By Les D. Crause

But we don't use it because we don't expect it to be there. We think,

"I have to use my own knowledge and training. I must now use my education and all the studying I did at Business School to try and make the business work."

The Midas Touch

God says, "Why don't you take my power and use my anointing? Why don't you let the gifts of the Spirit flow out from you?

I will prosper you and make you wealthy. I will give you supernatural ability and make you more efficient than you ever were before. Everything you touch will prosper and you will get the spiritual Midas touch."

Do you know the story of the Midas touch? King Midas, according to that old story, was the guy who became so greedy that he wanted everything he touched to turn to gold.

Someone gave him that power so that every time he touched something it would turn to gold.

It was awesome. He just went around touching things, until one day his daughter came running to him and said,

"Hello daddy, give me a kiss."

When that happened she turned to gold. That wasn't such a blessing after all.

Well God has given us a better Midas anointing than that. He has given us an anointing that whatever we do will prosper and be blessed by the Lord.

Supernatural Skills and Abilities

God will give us skills that we can use for Him. That is the bottom line isn't it?

The ultimate goal is the extension of the Kingdom of God. But that anointing does not have to be confined to your preaching and your ministry abilities.

That anointing of God can be involved in every single thing you do, whether it be artistic expression, creating new products, or any new idea or anything that you do with your hands.

You might say, "So where is it in the Bible?"

You know we get these diehard analyticals who say,

"I want chapter and verse please."

Well here is a passage for you. Exodus 31:1 to 5 says,

And the LORD [Yahweh] spoke to Moses, saying, See, I have called by name Bezaleel the son of Uri, the son of Hur, of the tribe of Judah:

And I have filled him with the spirit of God, in wisdom, and in understanding, and in knowledge, and in all manner of workmanship,
To devise cunning works, to work in gold, and in silver, and in brass,
And in cutting of stones, to set [them], and in carving of timber, to work in all manner of workmanship.

This guy excelled in everything he touched. I mean he didn't just work in gold. He worked in silver and brass, stones and wood, and everything he touched he did by the power of God. He was the one chosen by God to make half of the tabernacle.

God's power is available to make us excel in the workplace, but we've brushed it aside and said,

"It's not spiritual. It's carnal and worldly. How can I bring the Lord into the workplace?"

The Lord wants to anoint you as much in your daily job as He wants to anoint you when you go to church; and as much as He wants to anoint you when you share His Word with others.

Functioning in Business

When you focus that anointing it produces business functions.

On the ministry side we saw that when you took the gifts of the Spirit and focused them, they all began to lead to specific ministry functions. We saw in 1 Corinthians 12 that it leads to teaching, ministering, and prophesying.

We saw the different kinds of ministries that all involve the different kinds of gifts. We use the power of God, and as we add the gifts to those normal functions, those functions become ministries.

We do exactly the same with this business anointing. It is the same gifts of the Spirit isn't it?

Yes it is. Nothing has changed. It is the same Holy Spirit and the same supernatural power of God. The only difference is that you are adding those gifts now to your day by day functions in the workplace.

As you continue to work on those functions in the kind of thing that you are qualified in, love doing and are passionate about, what happens when you do that in ministry?

God starts to focus you into a more specialized realm of ministry that eventually builds you up into ministry leadership offices. You have the Fivefold Ministry of apostle, prophet, evangelist, pastor and teacher.

Well the exact same thing will happen as you take God's power and use it in the workplace.

As you let the business anointing flow through you, God will begin to focus you upwards into higher levels of

By Les D. Crause

function and higher levels of leadership, not in ministry but in business as a business leader.

You say, "Now I'm definitely going secular. This is going outside of the church, because the elders of the church and the pastors, preachers, apostles and prophets do everything in the church. How am I now going to be functioning in business?"

You now become a business leader - an entrepreneur. You become a business owner who uses the power of God, and God lifts you up.

It is a combination of spiritual gifts and work functions. And just like a combination of spiritual gifts and ministry functions, it leads to the Fivefold Ministry offices.

Chapter 13

Ministry and Business Flowing Together

Chapter 13 – Ministry and Business Flowing Together

On the ministry side Paul gave us a description in Ephesians 4:11 to 13 where he said,

And He Himself gave some apostles, and some prophets; and some evangelists; and some pastors and teachers; For the equipping of the saints, for the work of the ministry, for the building up of the body of Christ: Till we all arrive at unanimous agreement concerning the faith, and the knowledge of the Son of God, to a mature man, to the level of maturity of the complete Christ:

One of the biggest mistakes that people have made through the years, is to think that ministry must be carried out by full time ministers.

We are sometimes still guilty of that. The idea of going into ministry full time as a career or job if you like, is so that we can now devote ourselves completely to doing the work of the ministry.

Under the status quo church system this meant that you actually did it as a job and were paid a salary for it. It was your responsibility to make sure that you preached at the Sunday services.

You did the mid-week Bible study and visited everyone in their homes. You kept everyone happy because that was your job.

Your job was to do the work of the ministry. And if you were called to be a prophet, your job was to prophesy over people and give them revelation about whether they were going to be wealthy or not; about what was going to happen to them in the future.

Role of the Saints

We have it all wrong. That is not what Paul says the Fivefold Ministry was given for. He said it was given to equip the saints.

Who are the saints? They are the ordinary Joes; every single ordinary believer who doesn't have any special calling that he is aware of. He is just an ordinary member in the body of Christ.

The leadership ministries were given specifically to equip, to prepare, to give direction and to train the saints. Why?

Is it so that the saints can pay more money to the preacher? Is it to fill up the pews so he doesn't have to preach to empty seats? No, it is so that they can do the work of the ministry.

So now if God has called you to be a Fivefold Entrepreneurs or Fivefold Business leader, does that make any difference?

By Les D. Crause

Chapter 13

You might say, "Well God has called me to be a business leader so that I can make a lot of money for the church."

No that is wrong. Who is going to make the money for the church? Who's going to do the work of business and bring it all in? The saints are going to do it.

How do you think the early church grew? Were all the big businesses donating their millions? No, the ordinary saints said,

"Hey, I have a house. I'll sell it and give the money to the church."

Or, "I'm going to sell my car. We have two of them and we don't need the second one. We will sell it and give it to the church."

The money came from the saints. But the problem was the saints didn't know how to make money so the church became poor.

The saints did not have business opportunities with Christian bosses, and there were no Christian businesses and companies to function in.

Also the saints were not taught to function under the business anointing and to be able to accumulate more wealth than unbelievers.

Equipping Saints for Business

That is why in this end times in which we live, God is raising up His business leaders to do what? Here is my version of this verse:

And he himself is giving fivefold entrepreneurs, for the equipping of the saints for the work of business.

Why?

For the building up of the body of Christ.

We cannot build the church without money. We need those financial resources.

God's people are suffering and struggling, and many have even turned their backs on the Lord and gone into the world because God didn't come up with the deal. He didn't provide the money.

You say, "You know I gave all my money to the church and believed God and we nearly starved. What was the point?"

That is all that preachers teach; that prosperity is just giving all your money to the work.

They are not standing up under the power of God and with the business anointing, and teaching God's people how to excel in business.

By Les D. Crause

They are not teaching people how to start their own businesses. They are not showing them how to sell better, to make more money and to accumulate wealth so that the church can have an abundance.

But in these last days God is raising up His Fivefold Entrepreneurs who are going to function under the business anointing.

They are going to become leaders in the body of Christ. And yes many of them will start their own businesses but they don't have to.

Failure in the Church

The Fivefold Entrepreneurs are there to teach the saints. Many of them will set up Training Schools in order to teach the saints how to excel in business.

Why should we go to worldly universities where we are taught against God, to try and learn the principles of business and making money?

Why is the church not establishing this? Why is it not offering training for business?

We just offer Bible School training for those who want to go into full time ministry. Why aren't we offering Business School training?

Everyone runs to the Business Schools and gets programmed with Pharaoh's way and the World System on how to make money in a selfish way. They are taught how to cheat people so that they can make money Satan's way.

The body of Christ is not being taught how to take the power and anointing of God, and get from this world all the resources that God has for us. It is going to take the Fivefold Entrepreneurs to do this.

They are God's entrepreneurs. They are chosen by God to lead the church in business. They are not called to bring money into the church no more than the minister is called to do the work of the ministry.

Yes the minister does the work of the ministry. Yes a lot of people get saved in church when the minister stands up and preaches the gospel.

But that is not where people should be getting saved. They should be getting saved out there in the world.

The leaders should be training the saints to get out there and to use the anointing of God to reach the world for Christ. They should be going out, counseling and ministering to one another, and praying healing for one another.

But we wait for the hour of power. We wait for the man of God to stand up there, and he is the only one who can do it. He must lay hands on everyone and speak forth the anointing.

By Les D. Crause

The church has messed it up, and it has messed it up even more when it comes to business. If God has called you to be a Fivefold Entrepreneur, what are you doing to equip the saints for the work of business?

Training for Every Area

What are you doing to create job opportunities for Christians? Are you teaching them to rise up and develop their abilities? Are you showing them how to tap into the power that is in their spirits?

The world says,

"We'll find whether you have a gift and then we'll use it."

If you were born with a natural singing voice obviously you're going to become a singer. If you were born with the ability to use your hands then obviously your job is going to involve using your hands.

We don't have to be stuck with that, because we know that within the human spirit, anointed by God's Holy Spirit, any ability can be developed.

You might say, "Lord what shall I do?"

He says, "I want you to become a graphic artist."

"But Lord I can't draw a straight line with a ruler."

"So what? Who asked you to have natural ability?"

Ministry and Business Flowing Together

Or maybe He says,

"I want you to do crafts with your hands."

"Lord you know I've been a pen pusher all my life. Clerical work is all I can do. If you give me a hammer I don't even know which hand to hold it in. Nails - what do you do with those things? A saw? That's dangerous."

What is God calling you to do and what really burns in you?

You say, "You know I always wanted to be able to fly a plane, but I just don't have the ability."

Or, "I always wanted to do that kind of job, but you know I'm not qualified. I don't have the training."

Well then start your own business and do it.

"I don't know how to start a business. I haven't been to Business School."

It is time the church offers all of these things to the body of Christ: qualified training, prophetic direction, revelation from God, teaching and all the resources that are needed.

The Fivefold Entrepreneurs are called to train the saints to bring in the wealth. Their function is absolutely essential for the building up of the local churches and for the building up of ministry centers.

By Les D. Crause

We will be teaching a lot more on ministry centers even though we have taught on it in the past.

The World Looking to the Church

It is time that the ministry and business anointings flow together to build the church. We can then reach out and take this world for the Lord, until eventually the world will start coming to us for business advice.

You might say, "I have never been to Business School and I haven't studied all those fancy things."

"Yes but you are making a lot of money. It seems to me that your business is flourishing right in the middle of a recession. What is going on? How are you doing it?"

"Well I have a key. It's called the anointing of God."

"The what?"

"The anointing of God."

"What is that? I've never heard of it."

"Come on in and we'll show you."

First he needs to get saved. Then you can do it.

You Can Do Both

You say, "If I am called to the business anointing surely I can't minister?"

It's like saying, "If I'm called to the ministry surely I can't do business?"

It is the same Spirit and you can do both. Yes, some will get focused towards the ministry leadership. Others will get focused towards the business entrepreneur leadership. These two will work side by side.

The Fivefold Business leaders and the Fivefold Ministry leaders will function together, complementing one another, overlapping each other and building the church of the future that the Lord has for us.

So in conclusion, there is an anointing available to all believers for the purpose of business. And there are various business functions in the body of Christ. Today God is raising up business leaders to bring the church to its final glory.

No matter where you stand and no matter what your calling is, there is an anointing that is just for you. And whether you function in ministry or whether you function in business, you are going to do it best if you do it with the anointing of God.

By Les D. Crause

Section 05 - The Fivefold Entrepreneur

CHAPTER 14

Different Types of Business Entrepreneurs

Section 05 - The Fivefold Entrepreneur

Chapter 14 – Different Types of Business Entrepreneurs

There are always 3 kinds of people in this world. They are:

1. Firstly leaders
2. Secondly followers
3. Thirdly losers

To coin an old expression, there are those who make things happen. There are those who watch things happen. And there are those who say,

"What happened?"

The trouble is if you are neither leading nor following and just going along day by day without any direction, you are destined to become a loser.

Qualifications of Leaders

If you're a follower, then you should be finding the right leader to follow. And if you are a leader, then it is time to step out and lead the way.

Different Types of Business Entrepreneurs

So in this section I want to speak to the leaders. They are the ones who make things happen, and they are the ones who lead the way for others to follow. These are the men and women who fulfill the following qualifications.

1. They have been anointed by God for business.
2. They have learned how to function in business.
3. Thirdly they desire to lead others in business.

If you have those qualifications, then the chances are that you are called to be one of God's entrepreneurs.

God's entrepreneurs fit into a very similar pattern to the Fivefold Ministry, so I want to look here at the Fivefold Business offices.

We have covered the Fivefold Ministry in a lot of detail in all of the ministry courses. Now I want to show you that there is also a Fivefold Business office.

I would like to give you a description of Fivefold Entrepreneurs. I want to show you what they look like, what they do, and how they are prepared and trained. And perhaps by the time I'm finished you will be able to say,

"Okay I know where I fit."

Or you will say,

"I think I'm a loser."

By Les D. Crause

Hopefully that will not be your conclusion, but you should fit somewhere into one of these areas. And if you don't fit into any of the five don't worry about it. You are probably just called to ministry instead of business.

The Evangelistic Entrepreneur

Let's start with the first Fivefold Business office. We'll start at what would normally be the bottom in ministry order, and that is the Evangelistic Entrepreneur.

The Fivefold Business offices function in a very similar way to the Fivefold Ministry offices.

They use very similar anointings and very similar functions. The only difference is that the effect they are going to create in the end will not be for ministry.

So just as the Fivefold Ministry evangelist brings souls to the Lord without too much effort, so the Fivefold Entrepreneur in business brings in sales. He brings products and customers into the business.

How does the evangelist normally do this? It's not so much by the skill of delivery. It is not that he has the right way of selling. It is because he has an anointing, a passion, and the faith to believe for souls.

Have you ever seen a true Evangelistic Ministry in operation?

If you have you will see that sometimes their preaching really is pretty empty and doesn't cover very much. But when it comes to that moment of decision and they begin to make the appeal, people get saved.

Well the Evangelistic Entrepreneur is going to work in exactly the same way. It is not so much whether you have learned all the selling skills correctly, or if you laid it all out systematically step by step and finally brought the person to a close.

Those are good things to use. But what ultimately makes the difference in the Evangelistic Entrepreneur is the ability to bring people to a close, to where they just want to buy and they make decisions in a business realm.

The Anointing for Sales

This means that this kind of entrepreneur persuades people to buy products. But to do it they use the business anointing.

It is still the Spirit of God and the power of God. But it is a specific anointing that makes people start to pull out their wallets and open their hearts wide to buy.

They say that someone who is good at this can sell ice to the Eskimos. Have you heard that expression?

You say, "He's such a good salesman that he could sell ice to the Eskimos."

By Les D. Crause

He can persuade people to buy something that they don't even need. It is a divine ability that God can give you to function in. But as in ministry, the Evangelistic Entrepreneur is not simply called to go and get customers and sales.

Remember that the purpose of the fivefold calling is to equip the saints for the work of business.

So the Evangelistic Entrepreneur must also inspire and train others in the realm of sales and in breaking new ground for business, because the evangelist is the first one to go in to break new ground.

So if we look at the concept of business as being a boat which I covered under my teaching The God Kind of Business, when the boat hits shore, the first one to go ashore is the Evangelistic Entrepreneur.

He doesn't do his work on the boat. He has to leave the boat in order to carry out his function. The evangelist doesn't function inside the camp but rather outside the camp.

And so the exact same thing applies in business as what it does in ministry. If God has called you to be an Evangelistic Entrepreneur, this is where your orientation is. This is where your desire lies, and this is where you excel.

So if you find yourself functioning and excelling in this area, the chances are God has called you to be an Evangelistic Entrepreneur.

The Pastoral Entrepreneur

The second level of course is the Pastoral Entrepreneur.

The pastor has the ability to encourage and feed the sheep. That's what a pastor does. He is a shepherd.

That means leading the sheep. It means protecting them and bringing them to new pastures. That is the function of the shepherd.

You see people need a direction. They are like sheep whether they are Christians or not.

But we are looking especially in the Christian realm. And just as believers need a spiritual leader, in the same way in the business realm, do not expect your employees just to know what to do to get out there and to function in business.

Even though they have a business anointing they need a leader. They need someone to give them direction. In business this is absolutely essential. It is a vital function amongst business leadership.

By Les D. Crause

A Business Counselor

Every single believer who works in business needs continual and regular direction. So the Pastoral Entrepreneur is a business counselor. He is someone who gives advice, counsel and direction to people.

The Pastoral Entrepreneur has to love people, not just love making money. In fact sometimes they forget that the main purpose for being there is actually to make money.

They love people so much and love helping them to get going in their jobs. And sometimes they forget that the main purpose is to make money, because that is what the business exists for.

They are so wrapped up in helping people, in encouraging them and motivating them to find their place and function, that sometimes they forget that this is a business function, not a ministry function.

But that is the amiable temperament that is in most pastors; the amiable that just likes to help people. So you have to go beyond the natural amiable temperament and into the anointing of God.

You have to realize that God has anointed you to bring together those Christians who are in a business function.

You must motivate them, encourage them, counsel them, and lead them in the way they should go in their business.

A Good Manager

The typical role of the Pastoral Entrepreneur is to be the manager of a business.

What does a manager do? He brings out the best in the staff. The manager sees the potential in each one, and tries to help each person to rise up and reach their full potential.

And so a good manager who operates under this anointing is concerned about every single employee in his care.

He wants to help them to rise up and excel in their work, and God provides the anointing that is needed for it.

On the business boat, this is the person who supervises the crew. He puts everyone into their place and gets the ship running tip top, with each one doing what they are supposed to do.

The Teaching Entrepreneur

We come then to the third entrepreneur which is the Teaching Entrepreneur.

By Les D. Crause

The teacher imparts knowledge and makes difficult things easy to understand. We know on the ministry side that the ministry teacher takes the Word and makes it plain for the ordinary believer.

In the same way the Teaching Entrepreneur takes the complexities of business and explains them. He makes them easy to understand for ordinary people.

Making Things Easy

If business was easy to do everyone would be doing it wouldn't they, because we would all love to make a lot of money? But not everybody can get into business.

Business is complicated and has so many facets of involvement; things that you need to know and mistakes that you can make.

You need someone to teach you and to train you in all the complexities of business - in all the laws, the tax stuff and the accounting.

There are just so many things that are involved in running a business that most of us think,

"You know I don't think I could handle that. I'll just go and work for a boss."

So we need someone who has the knowledge and experience to show people the way; to show them how to excel in business. Eventually he can bring them to the place where they can go and start their own business and function in the business realm.

Why must we do this? So that we can bring finance into the Kingdom of God. That is our ultimate goal isn't it? It is to build the church.

What is the ultimate function of the Fivefold Ministry? What is the ultimate function of the Fivefold Business calling?

It is to equip the saints for the work of the ministry, for the building up of the body of Christ. That is our ultimate goal.

It is not just to make money. It is to make money to cause the work of God to go forward and to be extended into the earth.

So when we come to the business boat, the teacher is the one that makes sure that all the right tackle and gear have been installed.

He makes sure that everything that is needed for this boat to function efficiently is in place, and that everybody knows how to use that gear.

The Prophetic Entrepreneur

Next up is the Prophetic Entrepreneur.

By Les D. Crause

The ministry prophet gives revelation and direction and opens new doors for ministry. What does the Prophetic Entrepreneur do? He helps people to discover their gifts and their business anointing.

He helps them to identify what business anointing God has given to them and what their business calling is. Then he releases them into their function by opening new doors of business.

Yes the Prophetic Entrepreneur has a golden key. The prophetic key is very much in function. This is a fully fledged prophet, but with an emphasis in the business realm.

The Prophetic Entrepreneur sends forth decrees, but they are sent forth for business.

He births new businesses in the Spirit using the anointing, intercession and the gifts of the Spirit, in the same way that the ministry prophet does.

The Prophetic Entrepreneur lays the groundwork for Christian businesses to be established out there in the world.

What is the role of the Prophetic Entrepreneur on the business boat? He is the one who plots the course and the destination that the boat will sail to. He is the navigator; the one who says,

"We're heading that way. This is where the ship will go. This is what our course will be and the route that we will take, and that is the direction we will follow."

This is because the Prophetic Entrepreneur has heard from God. He has interceded and prayed it through.

He has made a decree and laid the groundwork for this boat to be launched. And very often if the ship is launched it is the Prophetic Entrepreneur who will actually launch it in the Spirit. He will open the door and say,

"A new business is going to be opened now. We decree it and we send it forth in the name of the Lord."

The Apostolic Entrepreneur

We come finally now to the highest level - the Apostolic Entrepreneur.

What is the apostle? The apostle is a foundation layer.

The Apostolic Entrepreneur is the producer of new business plans and methods. We need the business apostle to move into new areas of business that didn't exist before.

It is easy to jump in and do what everybody else is doing. Everyone wants to start their own business.

By Les D. Crause

They see what other people are doing and they make a copy. They try and do the same kind of business and sell the same kind of products.

It takes a business apostle to say,

"I'm going to go and start a business that hasn't been done before. I am going to sell products that have never been sold before. I am going to produce a market that did not exist before and sell where no man has sold before."

That is the role of the business apostle. He is the foundation layer and originator; the one who starts something brand new.

How is he going to do this? He is going to do it with the anointing of God and using all of those other anointings.

This is because just like the ministry apostle, the business apostle is able to function in all of the different Fivefold Business callings.

What role does the business apostle hold on the business boat? I would say it is obvious. He is the captain in charge of everything.

So there you have the Fivefold Business calling. We always thought we could only do these things in church. But God is giving an anointing to go and function using His supernatural power in the marketplace.

This will cause the wealth of this world to come into the hands of the Kingdom of God, to extend His body in the earth.

Preparation and Training

If God has called you to one of these fivefold offices, where do you go from here? Well like every operation or function, it is going to require some preparation and training. It is not going to happen overnight.

We see people that someone prophesied over and said that they are called to be an apostle. Now tomorrow they think they are going to go and change the world and change the church. But it takes a bit longer.

We know this from experience. It takes a lot of knowledge, experience, training and death and all sorts of things, to come to the place where you are qualified to step into one of these leadership offices.

Well in some ways the training is different for the Fivefold Entrepreneur, but it is also very similar in many ways to what it is for the Fivefold Ministry. So I want to look at what is involved in being trained and prepared for these Fivefold Business offices.

These are the essentials for preparation and training in any realm, but especially for the business realm.

Accumulating Knowledge

Firstly you need to accumulate knowledge through study. You cannot do anything that you don't know how to do. You have to learn how to be any of these things.

Although you may know that God has called you; although you may know that the fire burns within you, you need some kind of knowledge, because without knowledge you have no materials to work with.

So you accumulate knowledge firstly by studying. We will look here at different ways that you can study.

Secondly you accumulate knowledge through mentorship. You need personal training, knowledge, impartation and discipline from one or more mentors.

They will take you and mold you, correct you and make you into the thing that you know God has called you to be.

And thirdly you need the accumulation of full knowledge through experience. It is wonderful when they take you through the training courses in sales. They can role play and they can give you the whole thing.

It looks so simple that a child could do it. Then they drop you off on the street corner and say,

"Now you go and do it."

Suddenly it is not as easy as it looked.

There is no substitute for experience. Until you have put these things into practice; until you have taken your knowledge and all of these things and translated them into experience, your knowledge is still incomplete. And so all of these things are necessary.

The Need for Wisdom

Then what do you do with all this knowledge? How is knowledge brought to life?

You know there are a lot of people who know a lot of things but they are still failures in life. It requires wisdom to bring knowledge to life.

Where does wisdom come from? We know that it comes from the Spirit within. So you must learn to tap the anointing of God and the Spirit of God within.

This will help to bring to life all of this knowledge that you have gained, whether it be through study, mentorship or experience.

Then as you tap into wisdom, you cause that knowledge and wisdom to flow outwards through words and actions.

Finally the ministry comes to life. It takes a bit of practice to say the right words and do the right things.

By Les D. Crause

It all becomes part of the experience, like opening your mouth and putting your foot into it. Or stepping out boldly and falling on your face.

These things are life aren't they? Whether you are doing these things in ministry or in business, there is no shortcut.

All of these things are involved in the preparation and training for these leadership offices in business.

Chapter 15

Business Training for Evangelists, Pastors and Teachers

Chapter 15 – Business Training for Evangelists, Pastors and Teachers

I am now going to take each one of the fivefold offices, and give you a few pointers on the kinds of things you will probably have to learn and experience in order to qualify for that office.

I am not going to go into it in a lot of detail, because I'm covering it all in one teaching in this section.

Perhaps later on we will have time to cover these in detail. But more likely we're going to be looking at that in more detail specifically under the Apostolic Business types.

The Evangelistic Entrepreneur

Let's start by looking at the Evangelistic Entrepreneur.

Not Much Studying Needed

What kind of study does the Evangelistic Entrepreneur need to do? He doesn't need a lot. All he needs actually is a basic knowledge.

Probably the most important knowledge that the Evangelistic Entrepreneur needs, is a knowledge of the product that he is selling and of the business he is representing. He simply needs to know what it is that he is presenting to people.

Yes a little knowledge of human nature can help, but usually evangelists don't even need that. They just go in where angels fear to tread and things happen.

They do and say things and before you know it people buy. It is just amazing how the anointing works.

The evangelist doesn't have time to spend years in study and get his head full of knowledge, because an analytical cannot sell.

So if you are going to be an Evangelistic Entrepreneur, don't worry you don't have to go on long study courses. Just learn what is necessary.

Mentorship and Impartation

You will however need some of the mentorship process. You will need hands on training from someone who is experienced in sales. It is not enough to know the theory and to go on a sales course.

You need someone to take you out in the field and say,

"Okay watch me and see how I do it. Now you try.

No you did it all wrong. Try it again. This is what you did wrong. Try it this way."

By Les D. Crause

Eventually with their help and with them standing behind you, you start to get it right and you can function on your own.

And then you need impartation of the business anointing. Where does this impartation come from? Just like in the ministry realm, impartation can only come from an Apostolic Entrepreneur.

So find yourself an Apostolic Entrepreneur and suck all the anointing out of him. Get from him all that you can and let him impart to you what God has given him.

Personal Experience

You will need to gain some personal experience. It might be good to have learned how to win people to the Lord as a Christian.

It is actually one of your best ways of learning to sell. One of the most difficult things to do is to sell a person on salvation. But it is a sales process; a process of persuasion.

Learn to sell your family members. Learn to sell your wife into cooking you the meal that you want and into being the kind of wife you want her to be.

Learn to sell your husband on getting you the things that you want. Get some practice in selling.

You know selling is a way of life. Every day we persuade people to do things for us. The process of persuasion is the selling process, so get some experience in it.

Have some fun with it. Practice getting people to change their minds just for the fun of it. Try and get them to go in a totally different direction, just to see whether you can do it.

It is good practice. Get some experience in selling before you have to go and stand at someone's door, or whichever method you are going to be using in selling, to get them to buy a product.

Having a full time job in sales is certainly a good place to start, because that is where they throw you in at the deep end and force you to sell. If you don't sell you don't eat, so you have a very strong motivation to learn how to sell.

You see if you can learn these things in the natural, then you are in a better position to receive that divine anointing and take it to the next level.

So learn, receive mentorship and gain some experience. Then take that anointing, rise up and become a leader.

Once you have learned how to do it then you can inspire others. You can take them under your wing. And now you become the one who takes others out, gives them hands on training and shows them how to do this.

By Les D. Crause

You get everybody excited about the idea. Not only are you selling a product, but you are selling people on the idea of doing these things. You are selling them on the idea of getting involved in a business calling for the Lord.

The Pastoral Entrepreneur

Next we have the Pastoral Entrepreneur. Let's look at what this person needs to learn.

Knowledge About Everything

The pastor needs to have a bit of knowledge about everything. The Pastoral Entrepreneur is not a specialist in anything, but he needs to be what we call a 'Jack of All Trades'. This is because he works with many people who have different business functions.

As a manager you should understand the job functions and responsibilities of every single person under your care.

How can you manage somebody in the sales realm if you have never tried some selling yourself? How can you manage someone in the administration staff if you are incapable of doing administration yourself?

So you must have a bit of knowledge about everything. You need to be one of those all-round people who knows at least a bit about everything.

You should know at least enough to be able to understand where people are coming from; to be able to give some kind of direction or to tell them where they can go and find more information.

It would also be good to have a bit of knowledge of human nature because you are working with people. You see you are not actually working with customers out there, although that is involved as well.

You are working with people on a daily basis and you are trying to bring them to a place of maturity. You're trying to bring them into unity and to build them into a single unit.

Learning to Submit

What mentorship do you require? Well perhaps the best place to start if you want to become a leader of others is to learn to submit to leadership.

You often see a leader who rises up and wants everyone else to submit to him. He says,

"I can't understand these people. They don't want to obey me. I'm the boss here. Why don't they do what I say?"

The trouble is they have never learned to submit to authority themselves. They enjoy being in this elevated position of being the boss, but they hate the weakness and inferiority of being under a boss.

By Les D. Crause

If you have never learned to submit to authority, how can you learn to exercise authority over others? So where can you learn to follow some delegated authority? Where can you submit?

Well you can start in church and submit to the leadership of the church. You could start as an employee by submitting to your boss and your immediate supervisor.

You might say, "He's such a stupid idiot. I don't know how he got the job. I could do it much better than him."

That is not an attitude of submission is it? One day when you become the boss, people are also going to say,

"What a stupid idiot. I could lead better than him."

They are going to do you the same way. You will reap what you sowed. So learn to submit. Learn to receive and get some exposure to this whole thing.

Learn From Their Mistakes

Watch and see how the leaders above you handle their staff. Yes you are going to see them make a lot of mistakes. And you are going to learn from that because you will say,

"I will **never** do it that way."

I hope that will be the case. And when the time comes where you find yourself doing that, your own words will come back to haunt you. You are doing it just the way you were done.

Haven't you seen how little kids take their dolls and start giving them a smack; the very thing they hate their parents doing to them?

They take it out on the toy. Or they take it out on the dog, because now they have a bit of authority.

We all make the same mistake don't we? Learn to receive from others first before you can give out.

Experience in the Home

How do you gain personal experience? Here is a good place to start. Start in your own family. If you are a parent you already have a team there, just like you would in a business. You are already a manager.

You say, "I can't stand sitting at home with these kids. They are driving me nuts. I want to be out there in the work situation, where I can make some money. I want to become a supervisor and a boss and lead adults."

Well if you can't lead children you won't be leading adults let me tell you. And if your kids are unruly and incapable, look at yourself. You are to blame. You're a bad manager. You are not qualified to be a pastor at all.

By Les D. Crause

You say, "I can't understand why God has given me such problems in the family. The kids are giving me such grief."

Perhaps it is preparation for the Pastoral Entrepreneur. Have you thought about that? God is giving you exposure at the closest level He can.

Learn to become a trusted friend and advisor. People should be looking to you for direction and counsel.

If you become the kind of person that people like to seek out for a bit of advice and encouragement, God could be preparing you to become that business leader. You will be there to encourage and counsel people under your care.

The Importance of Teamwork

Learn to work in a team situation. It is great being in a team situation where you are the team leader isn't it? But many team leaders have never learned to play in a team. To them being a team leader means,

"I do everything. I'm in charge and we jump to my tune."

You need to have learned to work in a team and be part of a group, where you add your little bit and everyone else adds theirs and you work together as one.

If you have never learned to do that you will never become a good manager or a Pastoral Entrepreneur.

So look at some of the things God has been putting you through. Then instead of fighting them say,

"Okay I see what's happening here. I get it. The Lord is getting the message across to me.

I need to get myself sorted out, because until I get this right I am not going to move into the wider responsibility. I'm also not going to be able to fulfill the calling that God has given me."

The Teaching Entrepreneur

We come now to the Teaching Entrepreneur. What kind of knowledge does the Teaching Entrepreneur need? What kind of study must he do?

Learn Everything

You need to learn everything you can lay your hands on. Read every book that you find to read. Use multimedia materials - videos, audios or anything you can find.

Consume it with a passion, because you are going to have to learn everything about everything. You will have to specialize in everything.

Learn all the extra stuff, like the accounting side of business, the legal side of business and all the complexities that go with it. You have to know everything there is to know about business or you can't teach and instruct others.

You will have to know those difficult things that most people don't understand. You see it is only when you know them and understand them that you can take those things and explain them in a simple way to ordinary people.

If you have this passion to accumulate knowledge, to learn and to study all these things, it could be that you are being prepared for this calling as a Teaching Entrepreneur.

Study the Word

Study the Bible very closely because you are not just an ordinary business leader. You are not running a business school in the world. You are doing this for the Kingdom of God.

And if you are going to teach business, it is not enough to know the laws of the land. It is not enough to know the way the world does business. You need to know God's way of doing business.

Study the Bible closely, and especially know every bit of teaching that Solomon gave because he was the ultimate teacher on business in the Scriptures.

You should be reading the book of Proverbs every day. There are 31 chapters in Proverbs, the equivalent of the number of days in a full month. Every single day you should go and look at the date and read that chapter from Proverbs.

Fill yourself with all the knowledge and the principles that Solomon had to give. Know that when you teach people, you will not be teaching them just any kind of business, but God's way of doing business.

Learn From Everyone

How about mentorship? Who are you going to learn from? You can learn from everyone you meet. Every single person that you meet in business is a person who probably knows something that you don't.

You might say, "I'm the leader here. I'm the boss and the teacher. Here is this ignorant little employee. What does he know?"

I guarantee that he knows something that you don't. He has experience and has been through things in life that you have not.

Always be open and ready to learn and remain teachable. Ask lots of questions all the time. Bug people with questions. Say to them,

"I have another question to ask you. Do you mind if I ask you another one?"

By Les D. Crause

Bug them, nag them and pull it out of them. Force them to tell you everything they know, until you know more than them; until you come to the place where you know everything about everything.

Attend lots of business seminars. Yes they are the way of the world and they are teaching a lot of things, but they have experience.

Go and meet other business people who have excelled in business, even if it is to learn from them how not to do it.

You must not only know **how** to do it, but how **not** to do it, because you must teach people. You must teach God's people how they shouldn't do business.

Show them how they should not follow the way of the world and do it Satan's way, but do it God's way.

And then get close to some Bible teachers, because the teaching function is the same whether you are teaching the Word or you are teaching secular knowledge. In any case you are going to be flowing in the same kind of anointing.

It is going to take God's ability for you to take complex things and make them simple for the people; to explain them in simple words, using wisdom that comes from within from the anointing that is upon you.

The Importance of Listening

How can you get experience as a teacher? Listen to people and find out what they are confused about. Don't just come in there with your great knowledge and say,

"I'm a teacher and I am going to tell everyone what to do and how to do it."

Teach people what they need to learn, but don't teach them to show how clever you are. You are there to help people to come out of their confusion.

Listen to people. Look deep inside and be sensitive to their feelings, and try and pick up what they are saying without telling you in words.

See the confusion within them. Then you will be in a better position to start taking the knowledge that you have and bringing people out of that confusion.

Share Your Knowledge

Share some of your knowledge with people who want it. Don't ram it down their throat and be an 'e-knows'. He knows everything - at least that is what he thinks. He's always acting like he knows everything.

People don't like that. They do not like you coming across making them feel like idiots. It's the wrong way to teach. Be sensitive to peoples' needs, and when they are ready to receive be there for them. Don't hold back and say,

"I know something that you don't know. I'm not going to share all the knowledge with you. This has cost me years of study.

I bought all those books, and went to University and Business School and all the business seminars. It cost me a fortune. Do you think I am going to give it to you for free?"

Yes because you have an anointing. It's not to say that you are going to do this as a business and charge them for the courses.

There is nothing wrong with that. I can tell you that I'm offering better stuff than the world is. They can pay a good price for it. You are in business after all.

How about building some web pages or putting out some blogs? Start sharing some of your knowledge freely with people on the web. They will come in and visit your site and get excited about all these things.

It is a good place to practice. If you offer it to people for free they will come and receive. You can then build a reputation and gain some experience.

People may stop visiting your site and saying,

"We don't understand your stuff."

If this happens then you know you are doing something wrong. Or maybe you just weren't called to be a teacher in the first place, but get some exposure.

You know you can't just go out there and say,

"Just wait till I get to church. I'm going to hammer everybody in business."

Your Circle of Influence

Who are you meeting? What people do you know? Where is your circle of influence?

Most of us only have a small circle of influence, usually our family and friends. And you know they won't want to receive teaching from you because they knew you when you grew up. They will say,

"Who do you think you are coming to tell us what to do now, just because you studied a few books."

You need to get exposure by spreading your knowledge out, and the Internet is actually one of the best ways to do that.

Get yourself some web pages up there. Then start offering your knowledge and people will come in and receive it.

If you are in a job situation, why don't you help some of your fellow employees?

By Les D. Crause

You say, "I don't have time to help him. He gets paid for his own job. He can work it out himself. Besides he will start looking better to the boss than me. I had rather impress the boss with my knowledge and he can stay ignorant."

It shouldn't be that way as Christians. Get some practice in your work place. Start to share your knowledge with others.

Favor in My Workplace

You know I was in a position once where my second level boss above me came to me the one day and asked my advice on something. That was quite awesome. This wasn't my immediate boss but the one above him.

He said, "Can I speak to you?"

I thought, "Oh boy I'm in trouble."

He called me into his office and said,

"I believe you are quite good at this and I'm having a bit of a problem with it. Do you think you could help me?"

I was in teaching preparation and training way back then already.

Look for the signs. Get involved and be ready to share openly with everybody. Get exposure and experience, and then take that anointing and get out and lead God's people.

Teach them how to do business God's way, and how to bring in the wealth of the wicked for the righteous and for the Kingdom of God.

By Les D. Crause

Chapter 16

Business Training for Prophets and Apostles

Chapter 16 – Business Training for Prophets and Apostles

The Prophetic Entrepreneur

Let's look now at the Prophetic Entrepreneur. What must the prophet study?

Watch Business Trends

You need to study the business market very carefully. You must learn business and cultural trends and watch what is happening in the marketplace. Watch the way business is going because you are looking to the future as a prophet.

You are looking for direction on what is the best way to lead the church in business, so watch what is happening in the world.

Look at what God is doing in the church. Watch all the business trends and be up to date with everything that is happening out there.

Watch and read every advertisement that comes your way. You might say,

"I'm so sick of these ads on TV all the time."

Watch them. Look at them carefully and say,

"What effect does this advert have on me? Why is it affecting me this way? I can learn from this. We can do better than that."

Learn from doing this. And then journal daily and learn to hear the voice of God. Because you see until you have heard from God, how are you going to give direction to the church?

So you must accumulate all the knowledge that you have about what is happening in the marketplace and in the body of Christ.

Involvement in Selling

Then for mentorship you must get involved in the marketing side of the business.

You say, "You know I'm not really qualified to be a sales person. In any case I'm in management. I'm one of the high leaders here."

Well why don't you go out and get some sales practice? Go out with one of the sales people and see how you can cope with a sale.

Let people teach you what they do. See the mistakes that they make so that you can give them better direction.

Work with the sales staff and learn to motivate people, because part of the prophetic function is motivating and inspiring people. It involves giving them a direction and getting them excited so that they want to go out and conquer the world.

Most people just carry on and do their job. But it takes a prophet to say to someone,

"I see that you are actually really good at doing this function. When you share with people I see them open their hearts wide to you."

Or, "You are very persuasive and you have a real ability there. I can see that God has given you an anointing. Are you aware of that?"

"I've never really thought about that. I just do it."

Isn't this the same thing that happens in ministry? It happens in the business realm too. People are not aware of their calling. It is for you to identify that calling, to bring it out and get revelation for them.

Why can't you go into the business marketplace and say,

"I have a word for you from the Lord. God says He is going to use you as an entrepreneur. He's going to lift you up and you are going to be in your own business. You will make a lot of money."

I wouldn't mind getting a word like that. Would you? Prophets are doing this in churches all the time. They are prophesying over people and telling them that they are going to become wealthy.

You don't have to do it in church. Go and do it in the workplace, but learn how to do it from successful business leaders.

Submit yourself to mentorship. Find someone who is good at this and who has succeeded in business and say,

"I want to learn from you. I want you to teach me."

Find an Apostolic Entrepreneur and get from them all that they have. Receive that anointing and an impartation from them. Get all that you can.

Helping People in Business

And then you need to get some experience. Offer to help Christian businesses to get going. Go out there and help other people with their businesses. Set up a blog site on the Internet and practice motivating Christians in business.

Get them motivated and encouraged and they will come back all the time for their 'fix'. You know we all need that weekly fix. Christians call it the weekly Sunday service, but business people need it too. We need our weekly fix.

You might say, "I really tried to get into business but it was so tough this week. The customers were heavy and the sales were hard. I just don't feel like doing business anymore."

By Les D. Crause

You need someone to motivate and encourage you and say,

"You know you really are doing well. I just sense by the Spirit that you are moving to a new level. You are going through some things and God is doing something wonderful in you. I see that He is going to lift you up and open new doors for you."

Let it flow. Set them on fire because that is what a prophet does isn't it? You can do it in business too.

Set up a mailing list and send out promotional emails. Get people onto your lists. You don't have to send out Daily Devotionals for Ministry. You can send out Daily Devotionals for Business. Why not?

Yes you can use the Word. You can show people God's ways. Get Christians inspired and motivated and give them direction.

You need to test the results to all your projects and look for some patterns because you need to give direction. You must know the right or the wrong way to go, so get some practice and exposure out there.

Going Through Death

You need to journal and do what God says. And when you have done what God says and it doesn't work then you heard wrong. So learn to get some practice in hearing God correctly.

You might say, "We plotted the course for this ship and went straight onto the rocks."

Oh dear someone missed it there. It could have been you. It is called prophetic death.

Don't think that you are going to escape it. I have found that for the business calling though there is not much death, because what use are you dead? You are no use to man or beast dead. You need to go and make money.

You could say, "You know I really learned by not getting any sales."

"So are you saying you are going to starve now?"

Nobody benefited from anything by you having learned how **not** to get sales. Go and learn how to make sales.

You say, "The Lord needs to take away my natural ability."

Yes, but He needs to give you some ability too otherwise you will starve. Motivation is very different in business to what it is in ministry, so don't keep looking for death all the time.

Yes you will go through the deaths like when you try and do it your own way. But God wants you to do it a better way. The whole purpose is for you to get in there and succeed, not to die all the time.

The Apostolic Entrepreneur

Let's look finally at the Apostolic Entrepreneur now.

Learn All About Business

The Apostolic Entrepreneur must learn everything that there is to know about business. As an Apostolic Entrepreneur you must get experience in all kinds of business.

You might say, "You know I can't understand why I've been through so many jobs. I have worked in every area you can think of already. I've done sales and admin, worked with my hands and done a bit of this and a bit of that.

I really don't know what I am called to be anymore. It seems that I am just to be a bit of everything. I seem to fail at everything I try. I have been through so many jobs now I just don't know if I'm capable of succeeding in anything."

It could be that you are called to be an Apostolic Entrepreneur, because you need to have exposure to everything and to every kind of business. You must learn to function at all levels of business.

You might say, "It's not fair, I just joined this new company and they started me at the bottom."

That is good. Learn how people at the bottom think and how they function. Learn the problems that they have and how to overcome them. Then work your way up and build up from there.

You know the best leader of a company is someone who started at the bottom as a mailman or something. Or he could have been the floor sweeper and worked his way up.

He went through all the ranks and can now do the job of any person there. That is the kind of person who is qualified to be an Apostolic Entrepreneur and a leader.

An Area of Expertise

Then you need to become an expert in at least one kind of business practice, preferably more. You should be an expert in at least one.

This then becomes your business expertise, and you are very capable of starting and running a business in this realm.

In the ministry side we saw that apostles will very often have a specific emphasis. In the same way in the business side you will find that the Apostolic

Entrepreneur very often has a specific market or emphasis that he or she excels in and masters.

Submit to someone who carries a strong apostolic business anointing. Ask questions and learn everything you can from such a person.

Try and copy them. Act the same way as them and do business the same way they do. Try and copy everything that they do right down to the last detail.

See if it does or doesn't work for you. Be ready to receive all that you can before you can rise up in this leadership.

Be ready to receive an impartation or a release from a prophet. It will be a decree that sends you forth, launches you and opens the door for you to move into something new.

The Value of Experience

You must gain that personal experience. First learn to be faithful as an ordinary employee in the workplace. Then try starting your own sideline business and learn how not to do things.

It's a good thing. Fail a few times in business because it is the best way to qualify as an Apostolic Entrepreneur.

No Apostolic Entrepreneur has ever succeeded the first time. You have to fail a few times. You have to mess it up so badly that you say,

"You know what? I'm just incapable of doing business."

That is good, now God can do something with you. He will keep you humble enough to learn until you come to the place where you can rise up.

Work with those who are in the other business offices. You must build a business team. You can't do this all by yourself.

Yes you are capable of doing most of the functions, but you can't do it all alone. You also need the evangelistic, pastoral, teaching and Prophetic Entrepreneur.

You need them all. And you as the leader will coordinate all of these together and build the most powerful business team. Together you will be the most powerful business structure in the body of Christ.

And then try and originate something new in business; something you have never done before or seen other people doing before. Get out there and do something new.

Your Ultimate Goal

So to wrap it up, how do business leaders function in the church?

I am not going to go into detail on this, but firstly your ultimate goal as a business leader is to become a business apostle. That is the top of the pile; the ultimate goal that you should be aiming for. To do this you must get exposure to all the other business leadership functions.

It is exactly the same as in ministry. The apostle can do all of them. So if you are headed for business apostle, make sure that you get exposure to all the other business functions.

Then when you qualify as an Apostolic Entrepreneur, you will take your place as a leader in the body of Christ, standing alongside the ministry offices. The apostles of ministry will be standing side by side with the apostles of business.

I am going to cover that in detail in the next section. But for now realize that God is raising up His Fivefold Business leaders in His end times church.

These leaders are going to cause believers to prosper and succeed in business. This will lead to a transfer of wealth from the hand of the wicked to the righteous and into the body of Christ.

The church will be equipped with both finances and skills to expand into the earth. Together with the ministry leaders, the business leaders will cause the church to take its true place in the world.

If God has called you to one or more of these offices, then it is time to be trained and released into your office.

Section 06 - The Sevenfold Apostolic Leaders

Chapter 17

Business and Ministry Apostles Together

Section 06 - The Sevenfold Apostolic Leaders

Chapter 17 – Business and Ministry Apostles Together

God's leaders have always suffered financial lack. The main reason for this is that they have become so spiritually minded that they have given up their true inheritance.

God has always had a promised land for His people right from the beginning. The lack that we have suffered has never been because God didn't want us to prosper.

The church made this mistake in the early years, by making vows of poverty and thinking that this was spirituality.

But God has always had a promised land for His people. And now He is going to bring His church to the place of final glory that He has planned for it right from the beginning.

It is so exciting that we are living in these end times, and that we will see this accomplished in the Kingdom of God.

How is God going to do this? I believe He is going to do it by bringing out His chosen leaders. Who are His chosen leaders? They are the sevenfold apostolic leaders.

You might say to me,

"I have never heard you mention the term sevenfold apostolic leaders before. You covered the whole teaching on the prophetic and the whole teaching on the apostolic, and nobody ever spoke about the sevenfold apostolic leaders.

"We learned about the Fivefold Ministry and that there were four apostolic types. So where does the number seven come from?"

We have to put a seven in somewhere because it is God's number. I mean four is not enough. We have to have seven because that is God's number of completion.

It has taken me a long time to find out where the seven fits. But I have finally found it and I want to share it with you in this section.

Under the Old Covenant, God worked through the prophets, priests and kings. In the New Covenant, God introduced a new group which He called the apostles and the prophets.

Throughout the Acts of the Apostles you read the terms apostles and prophets. And of course they had the elders thrown in there as well.

By Les D. Crause

But in the end times church God is bringing forth a new group. He is bringing forth apostles and entrepreneurs. He is bringing the full fivefold function in both ministry and in business which we have not seen before.

Mystery of the Church

It is a new church; a new mystery. Paul wrote about the mystery that was revealed to him. And even the early disciples and the 12 who followed Jesus didn't know what Paul was talking about.

They said, "What mystery? We spent all that time with Jesus and He never spoke about a mystery. Where do you come with this mystery Paul?"

Well it was not time for the mystery to be revealed until God gave it to Paul. And it hasn't been time for the mystery of the end times church to be revealed until this time.

However we as the final generation are living in the end times. And now the final church will be manifested and come to the glory that God intended.

The prophetic teachings seem to think the opposite. All those who have studied prophecy and the end times are speaking about the church going into darkness, struggling and battling.

They say that there is going to come a falling away and hardly anybody will be serving the Lord. And right in the middle of it Jesus is going to come for this battling, struggling and miserable church and take them out before they all fall away.

Imagine a husband coming for his bride and she's just ready to pack up and leave him?

She's ready to dump him and run off with somebody else. He would grab her quickly before she runs off with someone else, right? What kind of marriage would that be?

A bride is the most glorious and magnificent on her wedding day. It is the most beautiful she will ever look and she is that way for her husband.

The church is going to be glorious and magnificent. It is going to be something exciting that Jesus is looking forward to seeing and receiving. The end times church is going to be a glorious church and it will be led by the sevenfold apostolic leadership.

Four Ministry Apostles

Where is this sevenfold apostolic leadership going to come from? Well to start off let's recap what we have looked at in the past.

By Les D. Crause

Chapter 17

We saw that God has raised up and is raising up four apostolic types. And we have already seen the restoration of the Fivefold Ministry.

Then we saw the restoration of the Apostolic Office, and we saw that God raised up four different types of apostles.

In our experience we have gradually been seeing the manifestation of these apostles in the body of Christ. Although it is not fully there yet, we are seeing evidence that God is raising up these four different types of apostles.

We saw that there is a Moses apostle who is typified by the life of Moses. He is the apostle who lays the foundation of doctrine and prepares the ground for the church.

Then we saw that the Moses apostle was followed by the David apostle. He is the apostle who begins to build on the foundation. He sets up the building and brings out the plan for the temple.

After that we saw Joshua who is the apostle who goes and takes the land back from the world. And lastly we saw the Solomon apostle.

Solomon is the final one who establishes and puts the pattern into its place. And now finally the church is established according to God's pattern.

Four Business Apostles

It is wonderful to have these four apostolic types, but something is still missing.

Somehow the four apostolic types have not yet begun to bring about the final pattern for the end times church. This is because we have not yet seen the manifestation of another four kinds of apostles.

These apostles are the business apostles. They are exactly the same as the ministry apostles, and they are four different apostolic types, typified by four main Bible characters from the Old Testament.

Who are these characters? Well you would probably think Abraham, Isaac and Jacob are bound to be three of them because they all went in a row. But as I waited on the Lord He gave me a slight variation to those three.

He gave me Abraham as being the first business apostle. Abraham is the Apostolic Entrepreneur who lays the groundwork for the business calling.

Following Abraham comes Jacob. He is the Apostolic Entrepreneur who establishes the actual business pattern that the church will follow.

After that comes the Joseph Apostolic Entrepreneur. He is the one who overcomes the World System. Isn't that what Joseph did? He overcame Egypt which is a type and a picture in Scripture of the world.

Then finally we get Solomon. You might say,

"Hang on, didn't you mention Solomon already? Wasn't Solomon one of the four Apostolic Ministry types?"

Yes he was, but he is also an apostolic business type. Solomon is the Apostolic Entrepreneur who raises the church up to its final glory.

God is going to combine these two groups to form His leadership. Well four and four normally equals eight, except one of them is common so there are actually seven.

We have three apostolic business leaders and three Apostolic Ministry leaders, and one who is both. Solomon is both a ministry leader and a business leader.

Combined together we have God's sevenfold leadership of the church, bringing both ministry and business together under one umbrella; one leadership in the body of Christ.

Business First

There is an order of establishment that takes place and it is different to what we ever expected. Who came first? Was it Moses or Abraham?

It was actually Abraham, Jacob and Joseph who appeared long before Moses did. All three business apostles came first before the first ministry apostles appeared. I am sure that blows your mind doesn't it?

The business apostle actually must come first. Why do you think we are still waiting for the church to return to the pattern?

Why do you think we are still waiting for this new pattern to be established and the new ministry centers to be established?

Why is it not happening? Because the business apostles have not appeared yet.

The Moses apostles are set to go as well as the Davids and Joshuas. We even have the Solomons waiting in the wings. They are all waiting for the business apostles.

Abraham, Jacob and Joseph must come first, before the pattern can be established. And who came last in both cases?

Solomon came last out of all of them. He is the ultimate spiritual leader who combines both ministry and business together.

There is an order of establishment. It starts with business, ministry is added, and then the two come together as one for the final pattern that God has for His church.

By Les D. Crause

This is the pattern for the end times church. This is what we have been waiting for and have spent so many years in preparation for. We have wondered,

"What is missing? Why are we not making headway? We have all this training. We have all these pictures and the whole pattern. Why is it not coming together?"

We have been waiting for the business apostles to appear, because they are the ones that must go and lay the groundwork before it can start.

CHAPTER 18

How the Business Apostles Will Function

Chapter 18 – How the Business Apostles Will Function

I am going to look very quickly at these four business apostolic types. Hopefully in the future I may be able to get enough revelation to give a full teaching on each of them as I did for the ministry apostolic types.

For now though I am going to cover all of them and just give you a few highlights of each of them.

I want you to see that there are a few things that are slightly different amongst these business Apostolic Entrepreneurs to what there is amongst the Apostolic Ministry offices.

Abraham

Let's start by looking at Abraham.

Leaving Everything Behind

Abraham was called to leave his country, his family and his people behind. Moses was not called to leave his people behind. He was called to go back and get them.

One of the first signs of the apostolic business call is that they had to leave behind everything that they relied on in the natural. You will see this pattern in most of them.

I go into more detail on this in the next section on the Cost of the Apostolic Business Call so I am not going to go into a lot of detail here.

I want you to see however that Abraham had to leave behind his country, his people, his father's house - all of his family members. He was forced to let go of all family contacts. He didn't have a choice because God said to him,

"You have to let them go."

Starting With Nothing

Abraham tried to hang onto his family but that caused problems. And then he had to somehow prosper on the worst part of the land because Lot took the best. He took the land where all the business was taking place.

Lot went to where all the prospects were; to where all the products were and business was flourishing. Abraham ended up with all the land that had nothing on it.

How could he prosper? Here was the great big business apostle and he was sent into the desert as it were. He was sent into the land which had no resources or anything.

You say, "How can God call me to be a business entrepreneur and give me nothing to start with?"

It is one of the first signs that you are called to be a business apostle.

You may have nothing in your hands, but God has told you to give up the little bit you did have. This may be some of your family inheritance and resources, and some of the contacts that you have already built.

God says, "Leave that behind."

"But Lord we have a good family business that has been going for years. I have a good structure and we have some great customers; some contacts and people that I know. I think we could build a prosperous business out of that."

God says, "No, let it go."

"Well Lord at least in the country where I am I know the laws and the way things work. So maybe I can just do business in another city?"

"No, leave the country."

You say, "But Lord I don't know how people think in those other countries. I don't know their business laws or anything about them."

"Good. I don't want you to know anything because I am going to teach you what you need to know."

So Abraham went into a land that he didn't know and a people he didn't know. He had one little contact who was Lot, and the Lord said,

"Let him go."

Then Lot took the last of the resources and the hope that Abraham had of going to all the wonderful, prosperous cities.

These are signs of the apostolic business calling. If you feel that God is calling you to do something impossible it is a good sign.

If you think He has put you in a situation where you have nothing to work with it is also a good sign.

Changing His Name

What did Abraham have now? He had nothing but the Lord. Abraham entered into a personal covenant relationship with God Himself, and God changed his name from Abram to Abraham.

God said, "Not only are you going to lose your family heritage, but you are going to lose your family name too.

In fact your family won't even know who you are because you are going to have a different name. You're a whole new person and you must look to me and to me alone."

By Les D. Crause

Then God said,

"Okay Abraham, I'm not just giving you the promised land. I'm giving you the whole world as your inheritance."

Abraham said, "Wow that is quite a promise. How am I going to do this? I don't have a clue."

God is going to tell you how to do it one step at a time. God told Abraham to go and walk up and down on the land and have a look at it. He had to put his foot on it and say,

"This land is my land. I'm claiming it now."

Abraham went where no man had gone before. He laid a foundation. Abraham is the business apostle who goes in where there was nothing, in order to prepare the ground for others to come and build. He is a foundation layer.

Jacob

Then we get the second apostolic business type who was Jacob. Jacob knew that he needed what his father had. And he was going to get it at all costs, even though he didn't deserve it.

He was not the firstborn, so he cheated his brother out of his inheritance so that he could get the family birthright.

He said, "I'm not going to be poor. I'm going to be wealthy and get dad's money. I'm also going to get dad's blessing so that I have the anointing from him."

You might say, "I'm going to get my spiritual father to pour all of his resources into me. With that I'm going to rise up and prosper."

No Family Ties

Jacob received it all right, but he had to run for his life and ended up working for 14 years for a woman.

Some big hotshot business entrepreneur he was. He became so wealthy working for his miserable uncle who kept changing his pay.

He said, "Well at least I am working for a relative. We'll still keep it in the family a bit. I'll work with Uncle Laban for a while and maybe I will at least get some of the family blessing."

God had to bring a total separation there too. Jacob had to break free of all relatives, all family and all natural contacts and hopes that he had.

God's Business Ideas

Where did Jacob get all his business ideas from? He got it in a dream from God.

By Les D. Crause

In the dream the Lord showed him that he would take the spotted and speckled sheep and would cause them to multiply. God gave him a brilliant plan of putting some sticks up when they mated. So Jacob went to Laban and said,

"I'll take the spotted and speckled sheep."

There were probably only a few of them and Laban said,

"What a crazy business plan. How stupid can you get? Are you mad? Don't you know that the sheep hardly have any spotted and speckled lambs?"

He gave his uncle all the best. In the natural it was foolish. But he was going where no one else had gone before and was doing what nobody else had done before.

He was doing it God's way. And what happened? Before you knew it Jacob had more sheep than Laban.

From Jacob to Israel

Jacob was wealthy because he used God's plan. And God changed his name as well.

God said, "Jacob you're not going to be called Jacob anymore. You're going to be called Israel."

Once again he was totally letting go of all natural resources and all family contacts and friends. He let go of anyone that he knew who could cause him to prosper, and he became the father of a whole nation of people.

These are some of the signs of the calling of the Apostolic Entrepreneur.

Joseph

We come to Joseph now. It is interesting that Jacob didn't inherit from Isaac, who inherited from Abraham.

You see there is no family generation that is passed down. There is no spiritual fatherhood in the business call.

You do not receive your heritage even from a spiritual father. Yes you can be mentored, but you receive your mandate from God Himself and He is the one who trains you.

So here came Joseph. Once again what an opportunity he had. He was daddy's blue-eyed boy.

If there was anybody who was going to get all of daddy's benefits it was Joseph. He was in the running; Mr Smarty Pants with the fancy colored coat who thought he knew it all.

I mean dad was going to hand it to him on a platter. There was no doubt about it. He was headed for the big time. That was until his brothers went and sold him into slavery and he ended up working as a servant for somebody else.

Everything Prospered

Joseph had the business call didn't he? Whatever he touched prospered. Wherever he went people started to put him in charge.

Wherever they put him in charge their business started to prosper. And Potiphar eventually put him in charge of everything, because whatever he touched turned to gold.

Did he get that from his father? I don't think so. Dad spoiled him and gave him everything for free. He had to work for this one though.

God took away everything that he relied on. And eventually he even lost the opportunity with Potiphar and ended up suffering in prison. He lost everything that was handed to him naturally.

Mandate from God

What was it that brought Joseph out of prison to be the highest leader under Pharaoh in Egypt? It was the anointing of God.

It was the revelation anointing that was in him that enabled him to interpret dreams. That was what elevated Joseph. It was nothing that he had received from his father, but from God Himself.

Can you see that as an Apostolic Entrepreneur you are going to have to hear directly from God? You are going to have to get your mandate, and whatever God is calling you to do you will have to get directly from Him.

You will not be able to receive this by impartation. Yes you can receive the anointing by impartation, but the office is not imparted. The office is delegated by God Himself.

So Joseph took control of the whole of Egypt and then he helped the family. He brought them in afterwards and they were all still subservient to him. He was the boss man.

That was a switch. All the older brothers who thought they were the hotshots and wanted to get rid of him, now had to come and bow and grovel to him. I like that. The Lord has a sense of humor sometimes.

All your family thought that you were the black sheep and the loser. Now they have to come and bow to you and say,

"We need a bit of finance. Do you think you can help us?"

God will elevate His Apostolic Entrepreneurs in His way.

By Les D. Crause

Solomon

We come finally to Solomon. Solomon was a little different because he was a mix.

Of course he had the whole family heritage handed to him on a platter didn't he? His whole family loved him and worked together with him. No they certainly did not.

The first thing you hear is how his brother tried to get rid of him so that he could take the throne. Dad was lying sick in bed with a naked woman. That was great.

Everybody forgot about Solomon. He was just stuck there all by himself; a mommy's boy. His mom was the only one who loved him. Isn't it nice to have a mommy who loves you?

Solomon was different and he did get something from his father. As Solomon the ministry apostle, he received his spiritual mandate from David.

The Solomon apostle as a ministry apostle does have a spiritual father and does receive a spiritual mandate from his or her spiritual father.

And so David gave to Solomon the pattern for the temple. He gave him the charge that he must go and build the temple according to the pattern.

Business Side First

Well David died and Solomon was put on the throne and took over. But Solomon heard from God first. He didn't rush off and immediately do what dad said.

You say, "Well shouldn't the ministry apostle go in first? Shouldn't he build things up and raise some finances so that we can get the work going?"

Do you know what Solomon built first with all of dad's money? He built the palace.

Solomon set up a business and started to make money. He made far more money than his dad ever gave him. Then he built the temple even better than dad expected of him.

Solomon started with his business mandate first. And where did he get that from? He got it directly from the Lord. He came to the Lord in his humility and said,

"Lord I'm just young and ignorant and I don't know how to lead your people. I don't know how to fulfill this mandate that dad gave me to build the temple and get it all done. Lord I need your help."

God said, "Get into business Solomon. I'm going to make you wealthy."

Supernatural Wisdom

Solomon was not looking for that was he? But God chose him and called him, and gave him wisdom and abundant wealth and riches.

Solomon built up the nation of Israel. He made it the wealthiest nation in the world, and he became an expert that the whole world wanted to consult with.

People in high places were coming from all over to Solomon for his wisdom and advice.

Well were they asking for spiritual counsel? No they were asking for business advice. They wanted to know how to become wealthy like him.

He just displayed all his wealth for them and made them envious. The Queen of Sheba came to brag with all her money.

She felt a heel after she saw all that he had because he had so much. She tried to give him gifts and he gave her better ones.

Isn't it nice when the church can make the world envious; when the big business tycoons can come to God's Apostolic Entrepreneurs, feel inferior to them and say,

"Can't you just show me how you did this? Can you give me some advice on how I can prosper financially and build my business the way that you have?"

That is the Solomon apostolic minister and the Solomon apostolic business leader.

God is bringing a new pattern into His church. That new pattern can only be accomplished as He brings the Apostolic Entrepreneurs and the apostolic ministers together into one unit to lead the church to its final glory.

The Usual Church Pattern

Let's look at the pattern for the church. Here is the old pattern. The apostle starts a new local church. People start to come in, they give their financial support and the work begins to grow.

Leaders are appointed, more people come in and the work grows. Finances start to flow. The church becomes established and then it fossilizes.

God then started to change things a bit and to change the pattern. He began to introduce a newer and better pattern.

The apostle comes in and starts a new local church. He sets up a ministry team using the Fivefold Ministry.

By Les D. Crause

The church grows and the Fivefold Ministers are sent out from the local church. Other works and churches are established. The work grows and there is a fellowship of local churches under the leadership of the first main local church.

It sounds good doesn't it? But it is not the final pattern.

The Final Pattern

We have been thinking it is the final pattern under the Fivefold Ministry mandate and ministry apostle.

We have been thinking that this is the final pattern but it is not. The final pattern is bigger than that. Here is what it looks like.

The Apostolic Entrepreneur sets up a financial supply. Now that is different.

The Apostolic Entrepreneur comes in first. The way is prepared for a ministry center to be created. Now the Apostolic Ministry and the business leaders gather together as one to form a ministry center.

Believers are trained in the ministry center to function in their ministry and to function in business. People are brought in and they are trained.

Fivefold Ministers and Fivefold Entrepreneurs are raised up and sent out to go and establish local churches in the area. And the local churches that are formed look to the ministry center for direction and financial support.

They don't have to try and raise their salaries. They don't need to hope that they can beg and plead with the people to pay their tithes so that they can survive.

No, there is a center that is producing all the finance that is needed to get out there and start new churches any time we want to. It is there to support those workers if we need to on a full time basis.

We now have a ministry center feeding all the local churches. And once that is established the Apostolic Entrepreneurs move out, take some apostolic ministers with them, and they go and form some new Ministry Centers in other parts of the country.

They start forming new ministry centers in the surrounding countries until it spreads out throughout the earth.

Bringing the Two Together

That is the final pattern for the end times church. And it can only be accomplished as God brings together these two groups. It cannot even start until the business apostles or entrepreneurs begin to function and put it into place.

By Les D. Crause

This is because without money you can't build a ministry center. Without financial resources you cannot spend time ministering to people and building them up without putting pressure on them to pay.

You cannot offer the Word freely the way God told us to because you need income. But as we set the financial resources in place first and put everything in place, we see the two working together.

The one continues to work and bring in the finances, and the other continues to work to bring in the people. As we do this we build the Body of Christ.

The Final Result

In conclusion, the new pattern that God has for the church will result in huge growth. There will be no need for the church to find financial resources before we spread the Word into the earth.

There will be no need for full time ministers to battle financially. They will have spiritual resources available to give to the people, because they will not have spent all their resources trying to believe God for some income.

Ministry will now be offered freely with the full anointing.

Preachers will have time to wait on God instead of going out and getting a job. They won't have to lie awake at night wondering how they will get food to put on the table or pay the rent.

The church is going to rise up in the eyes of the world. It is going to rise up high, like a city set on a hill that cannot be hidden.

Unbelievers are going to be brought into the Kingdom of God, and the church is going to grow until Jesus comes. And there she is - the beautiful, glorious, powerful church waiting for His return.

I think He is going to take one look and get all excited. He's going to say,

"Dad, do you see how beautiful she is? I can't wait to go and get her."

That is the kind of church we are going to build. And we're going to do it with the sevenfold apostolic leadership.

By Les D. Crause

Section 07 - Cost of the Apostolic Business Calling

CHAPTER 19

Letting Go of Your Archetypes

Section 07 - Cost of the Apostolic Business Calling

Chapter 19 – Letting Go of Your Archetypes

Genesis 12: 1 to 3 says,

Now the LORD [Yahweh] had said to Abram, Get out of your country, and from your relatives, and from your father's family, to a land that I will show you:
And I will make a great nation out of you, and I will bless you, and make you famous; and you will be a source of blessing:
I will bless those that bless you, and curse those that curses you: and through you all the families of the earth will be blessed.

Everyone would love to be rich wouldn't they? There isn't anyone who would not want this. The idea of the business calling appeals to most people because they say,

"The Lord has called me to become rich. It's wonderful, I can actually blame the Lord for my desire for wealth."

Well if you are called to the apostolic business calling I'm afraid that is not the whole picture. You see the apostolic business calling is not just a call to become rich. It is a call to become a blessing. There is a big difference there.

God made great promises to Abram. He said,

"I'm going to bless you and make you famous so that you can become a source of blessing."

Becoming a source of blessing was the main key. What is this blessing? The moment we think about business we think about money; about riches and finances. I already mentioned how in the Old Testament it says,

It is God who gives you the power (the anointing and the ability) to gain wealth.

The word wealth doesn't just refer to money, nor does it just refer to possessions.

It embraces something far greater. It embraces spirit, soul and body - all three; the whole person. It embraces everything that is involved with prosperity.

This means that it involves physical health as well as possessions, psychological health and ability, and spiritual health and capability. All of these things work together and Jesus calls this living the abundant life.

An abundant life is a life where you do not lack in any area whatsoever. This is true wealth in God's economy.

God gives us the power, the anointing and the ability to become wealthy and capable in all areas of life; to be successful in everything we touch and do. So if God has called you to the business calling, He is calling you to far more than accumulating money.

He is calling you to rise up in the world and to take your place as a leader; as one who will display an image to the world of what God's kind of man (or woman) should look like. That sounds so exciting but I'm afraid there is a price to pay.

We can learn from the experiences of the apostolic business types that I mentioned. They were Abraham, Jacob and Joseph. Solomon of course was a bit different but he is part of that group.

What it will Cost You

In this section I am going to look at some of the things that you will have to give up.

I want to show you the price you will have to pay and the cost you will need to bear, in order to embrace and receive this apostolic business call if God has called you to it.

We are going to look at the lives of these men and see if we can identify the principles displayed in them. I hope by the end of this section you will know whether or not God has called you to the apostolic business calling.

You will have decided whether you are prepared to pay the price. And you will have made a decision as to whether you are going to turn tail and run or head for the mark.

Give Up Your Country

Let's look first then at what you must give up. We still start with the bad news first. What did God say to Abram? He said,

"Get out of your country."

You say, "I grew up here all my life. In fact I have never gone outside the border of my country."

Some people have never left the border of their county or city. They are in a nice little comfort zone there.

Why does God want you to leave your country? You might say,

"There is nothing wrong with my country. It's beautiful and is one of the loveliest countries in the world. Why does God want me to leave it?"

Letting Go of Archetypes

Well there are many people who have left their country and still didn't obey this. It is not the physical leaving of your country that is the problem. The problem with your country is that it has what we call an archetype.

By Les D. Crause

I preached a message at one of our early conferences called Building New Archetypes. I come from South Africa and I understand the archetypes of that country.

We have had people from Switzerland, New Zealand and many different countries that the Lord has brought us. But why do you have to leave?

You see people leaving their country but they take their archetypes with them. God is not saying that they must leave their country physically.

Well He might be saying that, and it is going to be a whole lot easier to give up the archetype if you get out of it. But it's not enough to leave your country physically. I tell you what people do. They say,

"Okay I will leave my country."

They even come to the point where they say,

"I'm prepared to let go of my archetype."

What is an archetype? I will just mention it very briefly here. It is a kind of a national thinking that is bred into you and is programmed into you.

They start building it into you from your first day in School. It is national thinking. You get it on TV and on the radio, on the news or in the media.

Wherever you are exposed, there comes a kind of thinking that makes you want to conform and be part of the group.

Every country has their own little pet ideas and ways of looking at things and everyone is built into this flow.

Why is this happening? Because the enemy wants to be able to pull one string and have everyone jump at the same time.

You see Satan is in control of this world under his princes of darkness. It is all laid out. Every single territory is under a leader, and the enemy wants everybody to think and follow a certain pattern.

So if he wants to steer the whole nation he can do it very easily. All he does is introduce something into the archetype and the whole archetype moves together.

National thinking is such a difficult thing for people to let go of. They visit another country and they are rooting for their country. They go to a sports game and they are rooting for their side.

Here is the mistake that many people make. They say,

"Okay Lord, I give up my archetype."

You think that you can rest now because you made a decision to give up your archetype. But here is what you decided to do.

By Les D. Crause

You said, "Okay I'm going to leave my country and go over to that wonderful land of opportunity there called the United States."

That is God's own country, didn't you know that? Any American can tell you that. You go to Canada and they will tell you that Canada is God's own country. Any person from any country will tell you the same thing.

Switching Archetypes

So what do you do? You step into the new country and you say,

"Okay Lord I give up my archetype."

The trouble is you take up the new one. You replace it but it is the same archetypal thinking. All you did was switch archetypes.

You say, "Well the Lord told me to leave my country so I did. I stopped being what I was and I've become something else."

This is wrong. I have seen so many people making this mistake. I have seen it in every country, but it seems especially strong when people go to America.

America is a wonderful country. It has great opportunities. But God did not call you to move and to take on their archetype. You might as well have stayed where you were.

When the Lord told Abram to leave his country he didn't say,

"Abram I want you to leave this country and go to that one."

In fact he left it kind of vague. He just said,

"Leave your country."

"So where are we going Lord?"

"You'll find out when you get there."

"What is the name of this country?"

"I'm not telling you."

It doesn't matter; it can be any country. That is not the point. The point is you must let go of your archetype.

Let go of the things that control you and of your national thinking; of your inbred habits and patterns and become something new.

We don't like being unique do we? We say,

"I don't want to be different to everybody else. Everyone is going to say, 'What's wrong with you? You are being disloyal to your country. Look at you; you're a traitor.' "

And we shiver because it has been programed into us,

By Les D. Crause

"Don't you dare be disloyal to your country."

You are not being disloyal. You are going to be unique.

God called Abram to leave his country, to leave his nation and his people and everything that he was born into. But God didn't tell him to go and join a new one. He told Abram to **start** a new one.

Can you see the difference? If you are called to the apostolic business calling, God wants to raise you up.

This does not apply to all of the Fivefold Business calling. I will address that a little more later on. I'm talking only about the apostolic business calling.

God has called you to go out and start something new. That is what the apostle does right? He goes where no man has gone before and lays new foundations.

Paul said, "I do not build on another man's foundation."

That was Paul the apostle. The business apostle has the same approach which is an apostolic call. You have to go and lay a new foundation. You have to create something new that didn't exist before.

You have to go and start a new country. No you can't do that, but you can start a new archetype. You can build your own new archetype.

That is the first thing you are going to have to face when God calls you to the apostolic business calling.

By Les D. Crause

CHAPTER 20

Letting Go of Your Family

Chapter 20 – Letting Go of Your Family

Once you have let go of your archetype God then says,

"You must leave your father."

For many people that is a blessing because they never liked the old man anyway. They never had a good relationship with him. You might say of your father,

"He was a miserable old goat. He never showed me any care. I'm quite happy to leave - and the sooner the better."

Well if you left with that attitude you actually didn't leave him. You took him in your heart with your bitterness.

You must let go of both the positive and the negative because even negative thinking will control you. Your father will still control you, whether your attitude to him was positive or negative.

Going Through Individuation

Under the ministry side I have taught that we have to face a process called individuation. If you are not familiar with this teaching, individuation is when a child gets to a place in life where they stop being part of a family and become an individual in their own right.

They no longer have family conscious thinking and programming. They no longer think or do exactly what mom or dad say, but they make up their mind what they really believe. Up until then they say,

"Well we believe that because our whole family believes it. Dad has always said that so he must be right."

You come to the place where you have to decide whether you think dad was right or not. Sometimes dad was right, but sometimes he was wrong. You have to make a decision.

You have to become an individual in your own right. You have to decide how much of what was given to you, you are going to keep, and how much you are going to throw away. And whatever you decide is going to be new.

It is very difficult when a man and woman come together to get married, because each of them has this programming from their own families. Now they have the predicament that says,

"Are we going to do it my dad's way, or are we going to do it your mom's way?"

It causes conflict. You come to a place of individuation where you say,

By Les D. Crause

"This is the way we are going to build our family. Yes I know your dad liked to do it that way, and my dad used to do it that way. But I don't think we should do it either way. I think we should do it a new way."

Individuation is making a choice and setting a new standard. That is the natural process of individuation. And if you haven't individuated from your parents yet, you are by no means ready for this call.

You must not leave your mom out either. When the Bible speaks of the father it usually speaks about the mother as well. Some mothers can still be very controlling especially with their sons. You need to let both your mother and your father go and leave them behind.

You might say, "Can't we take them along just in case?"

That is what Abram did. He took dad along just in case and God said,

"Okay Abram you are on hold until dad is dead."

Nothing will happen if you don't do it. The call cannot proceed.

Why must we let go of the parenting thing? It is because there are two things that come down through family generations. There are family curses and we need to get rid of those. The last thing I want is to have a curse.

The Bible speaks of the iniquity of the parents being visited on the children and on the children's children to the third and fourth generations.

Family Generation Blessing

We must break the family generation curses. I think most people have learned that already. But there is a bit more to let go of and this is the tough one.

What do I do about family generational blessings? What about the fact that I come from a whole family line of preachers? And now God has given me that call, just like it was in my dad, in my grandfather and my great-grandfather?

They were all great men of God, and now that call has been passed down to me. It is so precious to me. I'm sorry but if you want to enter into this calling you must give it up.

You say, "But it is of God. It's anointed, blessed and spiritual."

Sure it is, but there is no spiritual parenting in the business calling. The ministry calling is different. In the ministry calling you need to give that up as well but I am not covering that now.

By Les D. Crause

Everything that you received from family generations is of no use to the Lord in fulfilling this calling. I will show it to you in the lives of our examples.

So you have had to let go of family curses and you have had to give up all those good things that you got from your parents. They were really good things and they have been your boast.

You might say, "You know my mom was always so loving and tender and I have her tender heart."

That is good, but you need Jesus' tender heart.

Let Go of Spiritual DNA

You have family DNA but you also have spiritual DNA. What is spiritual DNA? It is something that you receive from a spiritual parent.

You say, "So that's okay then. I can give up my natural parents' DNA, but at least I have my spiritual father and mother and I can embrace their DNA."

I have bad news for you. Sorry you must give that up too.

You might say, "What? But God gave me a spiritual father."

Yes He did for a season. And under the ministry side it was very important and necessary, but under the

Letting Go Of Your Family

business side it is not. In fact it will be a hindrance to you that will stand in the way.

You must let go of spiritual parentage. There is no Apostolic Father in business.

People who knew me and were under my spiritual or apostolic parentage in the ministry side know that I had to make a choice. They had to make a choice and had to let go, and they ceased to be my apostolic children.

Why? Because God called me to a new mandate; the apostolic business mandate. And so I am leading the way on this and I am practicing what I preach. I am giving the full example.

So you must break the family links. You must also deal with bitterness and laws of judgment.

You might say to me,

"Well I have let my dad and my mom go."

That may be so, but in your mind when the memories come back, you still feel the anger, disappointment and hurt.

Get rid of it. It is a law of judgment, and whatever you judge you will be judged with. With the measure you use it will be used against you.

By Les D. Crause

You cannot afford to have a law of judgment in the business calling. You will end up poor and you will end up transmitting it to others.

You can't afford to have it in the ministry calling either, but I am speaking about the apostolic business calling here.

Let Your Relatives Go

So you have to let go of your father and mother; your parentage. And then you must let go of a slightly wider scope as well. You must also let go of your relatives. This must include all blood relatives.

Why is this? Because families carry their own archetype. Have you seen it? We have the national archetype, but each family has their own archetype. Each one boasts in their heritage and their good background.

We say, "Our family stick together. We are very unique and very special. God has chosen us above the other families of the earth. I'm proud to bear that name."

Family generation bondages are actually sometimes stronger than anything else. Families try to stick together. They try to control.

They resist change and don't want you kicking against it. If you do kick against it they say,

"You're a shame to this family! You've let us down by not living up to the standard that we set."

It is control, but the only person who should be controlling you is the Lord Himself. You cannot afford to be controlled by anything in this world.

You must learn to break spiritual links with all family. Every time you make contact with family those links are re-established. The bondages are re-established and you come under their control once more.

Once again these are general principles that don't only apply to business. They apply in all realms of life. But especially when it comes to the business calling God says,

"I want you to cut free of every single influence, because you cannot build a new family, a new archetype or a new nation of people while you carry the old with you."

Let Your Children Go

You say, "That's great, we have let go of mom and dad, aunty and uncle and cousin, nephew and niece and all the rest of them. Hooray now I'm free. Now I can just sit down with my kids and my family and we can get on with it."

No, you have to let go of your children. Do you know that the greatest source of curses that we experience is not from the people who are over us? It is actually from those who are under us?

If you are a mentor the greatest attack that you come under comes from your disciples.

If you are a spiritual parent the greatest attack comes from your spiritual children. Did you know that? There is no fatherhood in business.

You say, "But I'm going to pass it down to my kids."

Yes you could pass the family business down to your children, but you are not passing the business mandate.

Yes you are going to create a whole new nation as it were, and you are going to transmit what God has given you. But your children are going to restrict you.

You might say, "God wants me to step out in faith, pack up my job and go overseas to Mexico.

How am I going to support my family? How are my kids going to eat? What happens if we get there and there is no income? What kind of father will people think that I am?"

I have been there. I know that one. The Bible says that the parent/child relationship is always temporary. It says,

Therefore shall a man leave his father and mother and cleave to his wife.

Letting Go Of Your Family

The husband/wife relationship is the permanent one. The parent/child relationship is never permanent. It is temporary, and it is only there for you to impart to your children, pour into them, mold them and then release them as arrows.

We try to hang onto our kids for as long as we can. But you will have to let your children go and let them decide their own destiny.

You can focus them and you can teach them. You can give them all they need and all the advice, and especially as a father you should do this.

Then you must let them go and give them to the Lord. You must put them in the Lord's hands and wave good bye, otherwise you are not fit for this calling.

By Les D. Crause

CHAPTER 21

Letting Go of Titles and Offices

Chapter 21 – Letting Go of Titles and Offices

Give Up Your Ministry Offices

Perhaps round about now you are saying,

"Somehow this price is a bit bigger than I thought. You mean I have to give up all that?"

No, not just that; there is more. We are not finished yet. You have to give up your ministry offices.

You know that training you went through and all those deaths; the tough time you went through to finally make it to the Prophetic Office or Apostolic Office?

You say, "It took me 30 years of preparation, another 10 years of training and 9 months of hell! I finally made it. Now I can sit back and say I am in office."

Yes you are in office, but if you want to go into the business calling you will have to give it up.

You cannot hold the business office and the ministry office at the same time. It can't be done. You cannot embrace both mandates together. You must make a choice.

Letting Go Of Titles and Offices

You say, "Does that mean I have to stop ministering? I mean I'm in Prophetic Office. Do I have to refuse all revelation? Am I not allowed to prophesy anymore?"

No I didn't say that. You see there is a difference between office and function. An office is a position that you are appointed to on a permanent basis.

The function is the actual work that you do. We learned when we first trained the prophets that very often we were training people for Prophetic Office who could not even prophesy yet.

People think, "I'm a prophet because I can prophesy. I get revelation and I speak prophecies over people, therefore maybe God has called me to the prophetic."

No, not necessarily. You must always distinguish office and function.

There is only one exception in the apostolic business office and that is the one typified by Solomon. Solomon is the only one who shares both ministry and business. But not everybody is called to be a Solomon.

We will deal with Solomon all on his own later in a separate teaching. For now I am sharing in general about the business calling and the ministry calling; the business and ministry offices.

By Les D. Crause

Keep them distinct, and if you are in a ministry office and God calls you into the business office as he did to me, you must let it go.

I was Apostle Les D. Crause, the Apostolic Father of Apostolic Movement International.

Do you know how many years it took me to get there and to build that whole thing up; to get that reputation and name and to be known out there as the Apostolic Father?

God said, "Give it up; let it go."

So now I am not Apostle Les anymore. I'm just Les. It got worse than that though and we will deal with that shortly. You must let it go. If you are not prepared to do this, then forget about this call. It is not going to happen.

Give Up Business Partners

Next, you are going to have to give up all your business partners and contacts.

You say, "You must have contacts in business. Don't you know that? Do you know how long it has taken me to build up my contacts?"

I had a lot of ministry contacts. I had a whole list of thousands of people, and when I came to launching my business mandate I wanted to keep using this nice big list. Well I used it once. I gave them one final letter saying,

"I'm leaving. Good bye. If you want to join me, this is where I am."

After that time I no longer sent to the main list, until the Lord told me to take the ministry mandate back when my training was complete.

Working With Your Spouse

You have one main partner in business and that is your spouse. If you have a business partner and you want to move into this calling in business, the Lord is probably going to call on you to let that partner go.

Why must you do that? Simply because a partner has to share the same call as you. If you are to have a partner, that partner has to share this business calling.

Or as we looked at in the previous section on God's Sevenfold Leaders, there comes a partnership between the ministry and business offices together, and you partner together in the work of the Lord.

In the business itself though you can't do this. That is why both the husband and wife must share this business calling together because you need that protection.

Sometimes it is tough. The wife has the ministry calling and the husband has the business calling. She goes to

By Les D. Crause

church and he goes to work. They get pulled apart, each one going their own way.

You say, "You do your thing and I will do mine."

Sorry it won't work. We tried to make it work at the beginning. We thought that it was the way it should be, but God said no.

In every single case, those who were working with us that moved from the ministry side over to the business side had to make a choice.

They both had to either go for the ministry calling or both go for the business calling together, but they could not split it two ways.

So you will have to give up all your business partners and contacts that you relied on in the natural. And now you will have to build a new team, starting with just you and your spouse.

God will create the new contacts. He will create the new opportunities, because you are not just building a business here.

You are building a business apostolic mandate. You are building something brand new that did not exist before.

Yes in time some of the people you know will eventually come in and be part of it I am sure. But don't try and build this new thing on what you had before. I will deal shortly with what you must give up and what you will keep.

Give Up Your Name

Here is the final thing that you will have to give up. It is your name and that could be a literal name change.

God changed Abram's name to Abraham. He changed Jacob's name to Israel. I changed mine to Bill. I always wanted to be called Bill. All famous people are called Bill. It was just a fantasy of mine.

I always had a standing joke. I would introduce myself to people and say,

"Hi, my name is Les but you can call me Bill."

It was just a joke, but as God gave me this call He said,

"Okay change your name. You are no longer Apostle Les D. Crause. And the only way people will not recognize you, is if you change your name completely and become something totally different."

So I chose a name that had great significance. Abraham means father of many. Israel means prince or something that has a significant meaning.

When God changed their names He changed it to something that meant something. So I chose a name that meant something. It was Bill Yinaire because people respect a billionaire.

It was not just about the money, but it was a status change. When I started out I began as ordinary Bill. That is a big price to pay when people have been calling you apostle all the time.

The Lord knows we never pushed for the title. But this became necessary because people don't recognize an apostle if it stares them in the face. They have to be told that this is an apostle or they think,

"Hey John, my mate."

So we set a standard. It was not to exalt ourselves, but so that those who came into this ministry could find their place. But God said,

"Give it up and just become ordinary Bill."

You know Les is my name and people have been calling me Les all my life. Now they were calling me something else.

There was a price to pay for that. Don't think that it was so easy. But the name also carries a reputation. It can be literal but it can also be figurative.

Your name is all that you stand for. It is who you are and the kind of reputation that you bear in the world. You have built a reputation and people know you by that name. When they hear your name they say,

"Oh yes I know him. He's such and such a preacher."

Or they say, "He is such and such a wealthy person."

Just mention the name of any famous person in this world and you will say,

"Oh yes, I know that person."

Side Note

Apostle Les only used the name Bill Yinaire during his training phase, which was a time of death to the ministry road.

However on completing his training as an Apostolic Entrepreneur, the Lord told him to take up his ministry mandate again and return to his normal name. He therefore no longer uses the name Bill Yinaire, and any references to this name are now obsolete.

By Les D. Crause

CHAPTER 22

What You Will Keep

Chapter 22 - What You Will Keep

If you are called to be an Apostolic Entrepreneur, you will have to give up everything that you boasted in before and start again from the bottom.

But you won't stay at the bottom. There are some things that you will keep. You are likely breathing a sigh of relief that you are not going to lose everything.

Your Knowledge and Experience

Firstly you will keep your knowledge and experience. That can't be taken from you can it? You have learned those things and you have experienced them. You cannot take experience or knowledge away from a person.

However knowledge is not power as they try and tell us. Knowledge without wisdom is useless. There are a lot of knowledgeable, very educated people who are incapable of using that knowledge and doing anything with it.

Yes God will let you keep your knowledge and you will keep your experience. But God is going to give you a new wisdom that you didn't have before.

He's going to give you a new power in your spirit. This will enable you to take that knowledge and experience that you have, and make something new of it that you did not do before.

That is what the difference will be. Your knowledge and experience are simply building materials. You may have had a big plan for the house you were going to build and you said,

"It was beautiful. We had been talking about it for years. We had it altogether. We even decided the plot of land where we were going to build it."

Then God said, "Scrap it; I'm giving you a new blueprint. You can keep the building materials because you have them already.

But you are not going to build the house you thought you were going to build. You're going to build a different one that I am giving you to build."

You see you are going to keep some of it, but again you are going to lose some of it.

Your Gifts and Anointing

You can also keep your ministry gifts and anointing. The Bible says that the gifts and callings of God are irrevocable. That doesn't change with the business calling.

God is not going to remove the anointing that He placed on you. He is not going to remove from you the gifts of the Spirit that operate in you and even the ministries that you operate in.

By Les D. Crause

However He is going to call you to give up the appointment to office that you had. That is the only thing you will have to give up. But you will continue to minister.

If you have ministered in revelation or the gifts of healing or whatever God has given you, those gifts will remain and continue to function.

You are still a member of the body of Christ and you will still function as a believer. In the body of Christ you will still have a ministry. You are not going to lose your ministry, just your office.

But you are going to get something extra. You are going to get a new anointing for business. I have taught on the business anointing already.

You will receive something extra over and above. God will take those anointings that you have and He will refocus them into a different direction but you won't lose them.

Testing Your Individuation

You are going to keep the uniqueness that you gained when you individuated. If you individuated well you will keep it and continue to be the person you chose to be.

Unfortunately many people only individuate late in life. You are supposed to do it around adolescence and puberty, but most people only start doing it later in life.

When God gives you this call you may suddenly find yourself being plunged into a brand new individuation.

So don't be surprised if your whole life gets turned upside down and you are challenged on everything you have ever believed.

Individuation is not just a simple decision where you say,

"Okay we'll do it that way."

No it is a continual process and experience that can sometimes be a very painful one. Sometimes you have to agonize for a long time. You will say something like,

"You know I've always believed that way. I've always felt that that was the right way to do it. Now I am being challenged to change."

Wait until you have preached it from the pulpit and God says,

"Change your doctrine."

You say, "What? I stood in front of those people and upset a lot of them. I was so bold and strong on what I believed and I preached it and taught it."

By Les D. Crause

God now says that you must stand up and say,

"Guys, remember that thing that I taught you? I don't believe that anymore. It is wrong."

Result of Knowing Who You Are

Are you prepared to do that? Do you have the courage to do it?

It is not easy sometimes to change and individuate. But when that individuation process is complete you will be that person and you will know who you are.

And when a person stands up in that confidence and authority, knowing who they are, the world takes one look and says,

"We will stand back; lead on."

Do you want to see the leaders of this world? They are people who know who they are. They do not impose their wills on others and try to dominate and control people.

A woman can stand up, not as a little girl anymore but a grown woman who knows who she is. She knows what she has and she knows her authority, and she stands in a beauty and a presence.

When she does that she makes men stand back and say,

"Wow."

A man can stand up in that authority and presence, knowing who he is. When he does that the men stand back in awe and say,

"I wish I was like him."

The women say, "I'd like to meet him."

The world stands back and reveres the person who has come to that place where they have made a decision.

It doesn't matter what that decision is. It doesn't matter whether what they stand for is different to what everybody else thinks. It is a case of knowing that they have the confidence and the courage to stand up for what they believe.

They are bold and strong enough to say,

"This is who I am. This is what I believe and I'm **not** moving."

That is the kind of person that God has called to stand up and become His business apostle.

Your Personal Mandate

You will keep your personal mandate from the Lord, because you are always going to have your own personal mandate.

By Les D. Crause

This applies only to the Apostolic Entrepreneur. It does not apply to the Fivefold Entrepreneur. I want to clarify this so that it makes it very clear.

I am speaking about the Apostolic Entrepreneur with the four apostolic types: Abraham, Jacob, Joseph and Solomon.

These are the leaders and the apostolic equivalent of ministry. These people receive their own mandate from the Lord.

The Fivefold Entrepreneurs - the prophets, teachers, pastors and evangelists in the entrepreneurial realm will work under the mandate of an Apostolic Entrepreneur. Can you see the difference?

If God has called you to be an Apostolic Entrepreneur you will not take the mandate of your apostolic father, because you will not have an apostolic father. You will get a mandate of your own.

CHAPTER 23

Price the Four Entrepreneurs Paid

Chapter 23 – Price the Four Entrepreneurs Paid

Let's look quickly at the four apostolic types, and see if we can see some of these costs in their lives.

I hope to do a full teaching on each of them in their own right so that we can examine all the different aspects of what is involved.

But I want to look very quickly at some of what we have covered, and see if we can see some evidence in the lives of these men.

Abraham

We start with Abraham. God told him to leave his country, his father and his relatives. So the first thing he did was take dad with him and he was put on hold until dad was gone.

Next he tried hanging onto his nephew Lot, and Lot ended up being a lot of trouble. He was eventually a thorn in Abraham's side. He had to get rid of him and lost the best part of the country as a result.

Then he tried to do business the world's way. People often say,

"This is the way I've taught it. It is the way everyone is doing it, and the way I learned it in Business School."

Abraham went and made an Ishmael. That was the way to do it wasn't it? If your wife didn't fall pregnant you took a pretty young dolly, made her pregnant and had your son that way.

It wasn't God's way though because God had promised a new mandate.

God had promised a new child to Abraham; something special and unique, but he messed it up. He tried to hang on to family traditions and all the things that he had and that he knew.

Letting Isaac Go

One last thing that Abraham tried to hang onto was Isaac himself. That became the end goal of everything and God said,

"Let him go and give him up to me too, because it is actually not your mandate. It is mine. I used you to birth him, but he's mine. He doesn't belong to you. He is simply in your care."

So don't ever think,

"This is my mandate. It's my ministry and my business."

By Les D. Crause

It is not your anything. It belongs to the Lord Himself and you have been given the privilege of being the custodian of His mandate.

Jacob

Next we have Jacob. Jacob knew where the future lay. The future lay in dad's birthright.

He said, "This is where it is at. If I can get dad's birthright I am made. I'll be the first in line. When dad dies I get the family business. That is the way to become wealthy, and if I can add dad's blessing to that I can't lose."

But he lost pretty badly. In fact he lost both. Actually at the end of the day who needed what dad had? His father wasn't that wealthy anyway - certainly not as wealthy as Jacob became when God gave him his own mandate.

Once he had let go of dad and the family problems he went to his Uncle Laban.

He said, "I'm still in the family you know. Uncle Laban is pretty wealthy. He has lots of money. I'll go and work for him and get his beautiful daughters. I'll get some money from him and build up some resources."

It didn't work though. He was limited and restricted. In the end Jacob built his fortune God's way. God gave him revelation and told him a whole new approach to use.

That is how he built it. He didn't rely on what he got from his father. And strangely enough Abraham wasn't his father. He was Jacob's grandfather.

He received the spiritual blessings from Abraham. The Bible speaks about Abraham, Isaac and Jacob, and God's blessing and Covenant being passed down.

But Jacob was given something unique that Abraham didn't have. His way of doing business was totally original. I mean who had ever heard of putting striped things by the sheep when they mated?

God gave him something unique. It was his own revelation and he built a fortune from it.

Joseph

The next one is Joseph. Joseph was dad's blue-eyed boy wasn't he? He had the multi-colored coat; a special place. He thought,

"I may not be the eldest here, but you know if dad is going to give any of his wealth away it is coming my way.

Dad is where it is at, and as long as I stay his favorite everything will be great. I have everything that my brothers don't have."

Well he lost every last bit of it didn't he? He lost his country, his father and his family - the whole lot.

By Les D. Crause

What did he keep? He kept his anointing and the gifts of revelation that God had given him.

He did not lose the visions that God had built into him from early childhood. He didn't lose the anointing of God, but he had to give up everything in the natural that he could have relied on and that could have lifted him up.

He used only the anointing and the power of God, and that and nothing else is what exalted Joseph in the end. He was given the opportunity to run Potiphar's household, but even that had to be taken away from him.

He could never have built up and become wealthy using the means that the world had to offer. And so he was elevated in God's time and in His time alone.

Solomon

Solomon doesn't follow the same pattern, but he has a few things there that we can look at quickly.

Solomon had a spiritual father for ministry but not for business. And Solomon had to individuate from mommy.

I think his mother was quite controlling and was a strong influence on him. She had to be like that because dad was always going out to war and Solomon lived with mommy.

In the end she just pushed it too far and tried to get his brother to come in and take Abishag as his wife. She was the woman who was looking after David. Solomon finally wised up and said,

"Okay mom that's it. That is as far as you go. It is enough now."

We don't hear about her very much again after that.

Solomon received his business mandate directly from the Lord. He came to the Lord wanting wisdom.

He said, "How am I going to guide these people and how am I going to build this big temple that dad told me to build?"

God said, "I'll make you wealthy."

Well that was not what he was asking for, but that is what God said He was going to give him. God chose the business mandate for Solomon.

And so Solomon took all of dad's money, and all the resources that he had left him, to fulfill the ministry mandate. Is that what happened?

No he didn't do that. He went and built a whole new thing. In fact the first thing that Solomon built was not the temple but his palace. He actually fulfilled the business mandate first before he fulfilled the ministry mandate.

By Les D. Crause

In the previous section on the Sevenfold Apostolic Leaders I showed that the business mandate always comes before the ministry mandate.

When it comes to the establishment of ministry centers it is not the Apostolic Ministry that goes in first, but the apostolic business goes in first.

Wrapping it Up

In conclusion, the apostolic business call carries great blessing, but that blessing comes with a price.

If you are prepared to pay the price you will experience the wonders of this calling. Fail to pay the price and you will go through a lot of unnecessary pain.

What lies open to you now is to pay the price and head for the mark. Head for the mark for the prize of the apostolic business calling, because that is what He is calling you to do.

You Have Reached the End of This Book

There is More For You

Continue reading to see about more books from us which are available on:

Amazon.com

CreateSpace.com

GBM-Booksop.com

And through other retailers.

These books are available in both Printed and EBook formats.

Continued on the next page...

By Les D. Crause

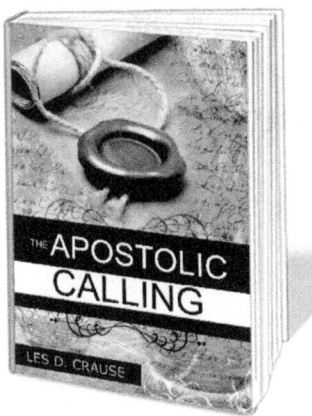

Apostolic Calling

Are You Called to The Highest Level of Ministry?

The call to Apostle is one the highest Ministry office that God can call you to. Very often the Lord starts to prepare you from a young age, and it can take years before you are prepared to flow in it.

God has been raising up His Apostles in these end times and they have begun to shake the church and the world.

If you want to be a part of this move of God, then you may have to pay a price, because there is always a price to pay.

But if you are prepared to pay the price then you could be one of the few that God has chosen to be His leaders in this world.

When you are done here you will know without a doubt if God has called you to this higher ministry.

The Apostolic Minister

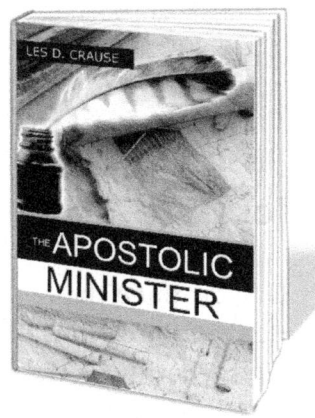

This book follows on from the last book in the series "The Apostolic Calling"

So now you know for sure that God has called you to be an Apostle. Where do you go from here?

It is time to learn the things that you can do as a apostle of God.

There are different kinds of apostles and each has their own area of ministry. It is important that you know which kind He wants you to be.

Apostle Les has given a foundational teaching on this subject to help those who God is training. Sharing from experience and examples from the Word, This book will show you where your true passion lies as an apostle of God and how He trains each of His Apostles.

Are you ready to minister in power and take the land that God has called you to take?

By Les D. Crause

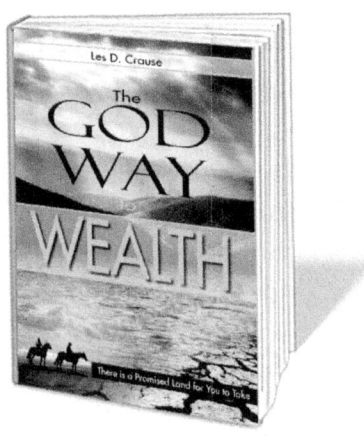

There is a Promised Land for Us to Take

God destined the Body of Christ to walk in prosperity and to take hold of the wealth of the wicked.

It has ALWAYS been His design for us as His children and He wants us to rise up and not be bound by any financial needs.

God has a Promised Land for His Church and He wants us to take hold of it.

Find out how you can identify and fulfill your business calling.

The New Way of Blessing

Parts 1 and 2

A foundational teaching and revelation by Apostle Les D. Crause.

Blessing is a part of you. You were blessed the day you became a believer in Christ. So then why does it seem that you are not always blessed?

This series lays out everything that you need to know about blessing and the spiritual life. How to discover and use it. You will discover the key to tapping blessing and what God has given you already.

It was previously one book but has been updated and split into two books.

By Les D. Crause

The Blessing Code

A Story That Teaches Everything You Need To Know To Fulfill Your Dreams and Desires

Everybody loves a story, but what if that story also teaches you powerful principles for succeeding in life?

Bill Douglas is a small time loser without a life. But all this changes when he finds out that he has received an inheritance from a distance relative.

The inheritance is not what he expects, but includes an old manuscript that transforms his life and causes him to fulfill his heart's desire.

Not only is the story one that will keep you reading to see what happens next, but it teaches you sound principles that could make you wealthy.

You Will Learn The Code For Success: The Blessing Code

The Way to Success

The Exact Stages to Follow To Succeed In Everything You Do

Everybody desires to live a successful life. But so often it seems that only a few hand-picked people really get there in their lives.

Does that mean you have to accept the fact that you will never be successful like them, and that you should stop dreaming and wishing for a bright future.

No! God has intended a wonderful future for you. He has given you all that you need in order to fulfill your dreams and to reach your goals.

These are the steps that you can take to start you on the road to success

YOU are chosen to make a difference with your life

By Les D. Crause

Look Out For The Twins

The following two books go well together and are know as "The Twins"

Using Your Ministry Gifts

When it comes to gifts and talents, you might feel like you were the last in line when they were giving out the good ones. And now when it comes to doing the work of the ministry, you still feel the same.

Why is it that some people rise up quickly into powerful ministries? It all seems to fall into their laps, but you and I have to struggle to be used by the Lord.

You Are Not Alone

Now you can find out how to not only find the gifts you already have, but obtain the ones you do not have.

Fulfilling Your Ministry Calling

You know that God has a purpose for your life, and a ministry for you to carry out.

But how can you find out exactly what your ministry calling is?

Can you do it by answering a questionnaire or doing a personality test?

Do you need a prophet to give you a prophetic word to tell you what God has called you to do?

No, all you need to do is go through this course to find out how.

Look out for these two books on the GBM Bookshop.

By Les D. Crause

Perfecting Your Prophetic Ministry

Is Your Prophetic Ministry Perfect Yet?

You can get revelation, but somehow it is not as clear as you hoped it would be. You wish you could hear better, speak better and minister better in the prophetic. Perhaps you have never flowed in the Prophetic and so wish you could.

No matter what level of experience you have had, this teaching will fill in the gaps of what is missing from your ministry.

And before you know it, you will be functioning like a true Prophet of God.

Prophetic Ministry Made Easy

A Ministry that is NOT Restricted to Prophets Only

The Prophetic Ministry has taken the world by storm. But there is still a lot of confusion on how the Prophetic Ministry should operate. Many amateurs have given this ministry a bad name, because they did not know what they were doing.

But God Has Given The Prophetic Ministry For Every Believer!

If you desire to step into all that God has for you and you have a hunger to hear His voice and minister more effectively to others, but don't know where to start, than this series is for you.

By Les D. Crause

Prophetic Visions and Dreams

Your dreams often have clear meanings. But when you try to understand them you get confused. Dream interpretation seems so complicated, and you do not know what all the pictures are supposed to mean.

You have read books on the subject, but they do not explain how these things work or why you are experiencing what you do.

You would like to use visions and dreams in your Prophetic Ministry but you do not know enough about them to be confident in this.

An Answer To Your Confusion Has Arrived

After years of experience in training Prophets, counseling and ministering to people using their dreams and visions, Apostle Les D. Crause has finally put together the most comprehensive teaching on this vital subject to date.

The Apostolic Entrepreneur

Reaching Prophetic Office

Find Out What God Expects from You to Be His Spokesman in the Earth

If you are one of the chosen few who have been called to the Office of Prophet then this course is for you.

If you know that you are called to this ministry, or you have been flowing in it already, this course will take you to the next level.

You will know what the Lord really expects from His Prophets and you can rise up into this calling.

By Les D. Crause

Functioning in Prophet Office

You Can Learn How to Confront Every Situation As A True Prophet of God

So now you know that God has called you to be a Prophet. Maybe you have even had experience in this area.

But how do you operate the way that you are supposed to?

How do you hear from God?

How do you prophesy? And how do you handle the rejection that comes with being a Prophet?

By Les D. Crause

Made in the USA
Las Vegas, NV
09 April 2022